GUARDIAN ANGELS

HOW TO CONTACT & WORK WITH

ANGELIC PROTECTORS

ABOUT THE AUTHOR

Richard Webster was born and raised in New Zealand. He has been interested in the psychic world since he was nine years old. He became interested in angels in his mid-twenties when he started receiving messages from his guardian angel. He was concerned at first, as he had no idea where the words were coming from. Once he learned they came from his guardian angel, he started learning as much as he could about the subject and has now written nine books about angels.

Richard's first book was published in 1972, fulfilling a childhood dream of becoming an author. Richard is now the author of more than a hundred books and is still writing today. His best-selling books include *Spirit Guides & Angel Guardians* and *Creative Visualization for Beginners*.

Richard has appeared on several radio and TV programs in the United States and abroad. He currently resides in New Zealand with his wife and three children. He regularly travels the world to give lectures, hold workshops, and continue his research.

GUARDIAN ANGELS

HOW TO CONTACT & WORK WITH
ANGELIC PROTECTORS

RICHARD WEBSTER

LLEWELLYN PUBLICATIONS
Woodbury, Minnesota

FIRST EDITION
First Printing, 2022

Book format by Mandie Brasington
Cover design by Cassie Willett
Editing by Laura Kurtz

Llewellyn Publications is a registered trademark of Llewellyn Worldwide Ltd.

Library of Congress Cataloging-in-Publication Data
Name: Webster, Richard,- author.
Title: Guardian angels : How to Contact & Work with Angelic Protectors / Richard Webster.
Description: First edition. | Woodbury, Minnesota : Llewellyn Worldwide, Ltd, [2022] | Includes bibliographical references and index. | Summary: "A book on working with guardian angels including exercises, prayers, meditations. Includes descriptions and mentions of angels in religious texts as well as famous New Age figures"— Provided by publisher.
Identifiers: LCCN 2022028425 (print) | LCCN 2022028426 (ebook) | ISBN 9780738770277 (paperback) | ISBN 9780738770512 (ebook)
Subjects: LCSH: Guardian angels—Miscellanea.
Classification: LCC BF1623.A53 W43 2022 (print) | LCC BF1623.A53 (ebook) | DDC 202/.15—dc23/eng/20220824
LC record available at https://lccn.loc.gov/2022028425
LC ebook record available at https://lccn.loc.gov/2022028426
ISBN: 978-0-7387-7027-7

Llewellyn Publications
A Division of Llewellyn Worldwide Ltd.
2143 Wooddale Drive
Woodbury, MN 55125-2989
www.llewellyn.com

Printed in the United States of America

Other Books by Richard Webster

Archangels (Llewellyn, 2022)

The Secret to Attracting Luck (Llewellyn, 2021)

How to Use a Pendulum (Llewellyn, 2020)

How to Use a Crystal (Llewellyn, 2018)

Angels for Beginners (Llewellyn, 2017)

Amulets & Talismans for Beginners (Llewellyn, 2017)

Rituals for Beginners (Llewellyn, 2016)

For my good friend Nick Belleas

ACKNOWLEDGMENTS

I'm forever grateful to the talented staff, past and present, of Llewellyn Publications who have guided and helped me over the last thirty years. *Guardian Angels* is my sixtieth book with Llewellyn's. The enthusiasm, friendliness, encouragement, and support from everyone has been, and is, incredible. I think of you all every day. Thank you very much.

Since I was eight years old, many people have helped me develop my passion for angels. I'd especially like to thank Nick Belleas, Doug Dyment, Tony Iacoviello, Jesse James, Sandi Liss, Robyn Luke, Darrell Mac, Mick Peck, Ken Ring, Blair Robertson, Neal Scryer, Jon Stetson, Luca Volpe, Alan Watson, and Dr. Jeremy Weiss. They're all amazing friends who've encouraged me in many ways. I am very blessed.

CONTENTS

INTRODUCTION

According to a poll conducted by the Baylor University Institute for Studies of Religion in 2008, 69 percent of Americans believe in angels, 46 percent believe in guardian angels, and 5 percent believe they have either seen or heard an angel (*Time* magazine, September 18, 2008). In the same survey, 55 percent of Americans said they had been protected from harm by an angel (https://www.baylor.edu/mediacommunications/news.php?action=story&story=52815). A 2010 poll conducted by ICM for the Bible Society reported that 31 percent of people in the UK believed in angels, 29 percent believed in guardian angels, and 5 percent claimed to have either seen or heard an angel (*Daily Telegraph*, December 17, 2012).

Angels are spiritual beings who attend to God and act as divine messengers. In fact, the word "angel" comes from the Greek word *angelos*, which means "messenger." The Bible describes angels as "ministering spirits sent forth to minister for them who shall be heirs of salvation" (Hebrews 1:14). Saint Thomas Aquinas (1225–1274), the Italian philosopher and theologian, believed that angels are comprised of pure thought or intellect. They can assume physical bodies whenever necessary, but even then, they are comprised of nothing but pure thought. Meister Eckhart (ca. 1260–ca.1328), the German mystic, wrote, "That's all an angel is; an idea of God" (von Hochheim, 1998). Dr. John Lilly (1915–2001), the American

1

neuroscientist and philosopher, believed that an angel was a "being from a higher plane than ours" (Jovanovic, 12).

Guardian angels are assigned to protect and guide people as they progress through life. Although they do this because they're working for the Divine, they genuinely love and care for the people they are protecting. Everyone has at least one guardian angel.

The fact that you have a guardian angel means that you are never alone. Your guardian angel works tirelessly for you not only throughout this lifetime but in previous and future lives as well.

Up until the early twentieth century, a common greeting among French farmers was, "Good day to you and your companion." The companion was the farmer's guardian angel.

The main purpose of this book is to help you develop a relationship with your guardian angel. You'll learn how to contact your guardian angel, learn their name, and work together to improve different aspects of your life. Along the way, you'll also learn some history of guardian angels and hear about people who regularly communicated with their guardian angels. I hope that by the time you've finished reading this book, you'll be communicating regularly with your best friend—your guardian angel.

WHAT IS A
GUARDIAN ANGEL?

Many people have tried to define angels, but no one has been able to conclusively answer the question, "What are angels?" Angels appear to be celestial beings of pure light who operate on a different vibrational frequency than us. Consequently, they are usually invisible to human eyes. However, in exceptional situations, such as when someone needs protection, help, or comfort, angels can lower their vibrations to a human level. When they do this, we can sense their presence, and sometimes even see them.

No one knows what angels look like, as they can appear in any shape or form they wish. If I saw an angel today and you saw the same angel tomorrow, we might have totally different descriptions of what it looked like, as it may have appeared in one form to me and in a different form to you. In the Bible, angels are assumed to be masculine, but they are actually genderless and can appear as men, women, adolescents, or children. People are more likely to listen and communicate with angels when they appear in a non-threatening form. In the Bible, angels must have appeared threatening; the first words they say to humans is "Fear not" or "Do not be afraid" (Daniel 8:17; Daniel 10:11; Mathew 28:5; Mark 16:6; Luke 1:12–13 and 30; Luke 2:9; Acts 10:4).

Many people expect angels to have wings, but they only appear to have them if the person thinks that is what angels look like. Angels do not fly through the air to move from one place to another. Instead, they travel wherever they're needed in a fraction of a second. This is why you can call on an angel and receive instant help. In addition to winged figures, angels sometimes appear in the form of birds or butterflies. It's also possible for them to appear as rainbows, bright lights, or in any other form they wish. Angels know what shape or form they need to appear in to catch a person's attention and ensure that they listen to the message and hopefully act upon it.

Some people believe that they become angels after this lifetime is over. It gives many people comfort to say that heaven has gained another angel when someone dies. However, this isn't the case, as humans and angels are completely different species who were created for different purposes.

This belief dates back more than two thousand years when Baruch ben Neriah wrote: "into the splendor of angels…for they will live in the heights of that world and they will be like the angels and be equal to the stars…And the excellence of the righteous will then be greater than that of the angels" (2 Baruch 51.3–5). Baruch obviously believed that good people became angels, but a special type: angels who were greater than other angels. In fact, the belief was that good people became angels who were equal to the stars. At that time, people believed stars were exceptionally powerful angels.

Belief that people became angels after they died grew enormously in the late Middle Ages, a time when babies and young children were especially susceptible to the plague. It gave distraught parents solace to believe that their deceased children had become joyful little angels who were able to return and give comfort to their mothers and fathers. This belief grew because about this time, artists began depicting angels as small, chubby cherubs. That said, it is very rare for a human being to transform into an angel. In fact, there is only one example of a person who may have become an angel: According to the third book of Enoch, the prophet Enoch was transformed into Metatron, the most important angel in Jewish lore. There are stories that St. Francis of Assisi became an angel after he died, but this has always been denied by the Catholic Church.

Like humans, angels possess free will. The best-known example of this is Lucifer, who was at one time one of heaven's chief angels. He wanted God's power for himself and tried to attain it by starting the war in heaven. He and his followers (said to be about a third of the angels in heaven) lost the battle and were expelled. However, the number of angels in heaven is still enormous. In Revelation 5:11, John tells how he "heard the voice of many angels round about the throne and the beasts and the elders: and the number of them was ten thousand times ten thousand, and thousands and thousands."

According to the Bible, angels were present when God created the earth. God asked Job: "Where wast thou when I laid the foundation of the earth? Declare, if thou hast understanding…or who laid the corner stone thereof? When the morning stars sang together, and all the sons of God shouted for joy?" (Job 38:4, 6–7). The terms "morning stars" and "the sons of God" refer to angels.

The main task of angels is to carry messages to and from the Divine. In fact, the word "angel" comes from the Greek word *angelos*, which means "messenger." The Bible contains many instances in which angels appeared to people with a message from the Divine. The most famous example of this is when Archangel Gabriel visited the Virgin Mary and told her that she was going to give birth to Jesus, the son of God. An old Jewish legend says that when Gabriel introduced herself to Abraham, she said, "I am the angel Gabriel, the messenger of God" (Ginzberg, 189). Gabriel has always been considered God's most important messenger, and in 1951 Pope Pius XII declared Archangel Gabriel the patron saint of postal workers. This means that God's chief messenger looks after the people who deliver messages.

In addition to acting as messengers, angels have many other duties. They attend the throne of God (Genesis 32:1; Psalms 103:21; 1 Kings 22:19; Job 1:6) and worship and praise Him. In Isaiah 6:3, the seraphim, who are important angels, hover around God saying: "Holy, holy, holy, is the LORD of hosts: the whole earth is full of His glory."

Angels are sometimes called upon to control the forces of nature. St. John the Divine wrote: "I saw four angels standing on the four corners of the earth, holding the four winds of the earth, that the wind should not blow on the earth, nor on the sea, nor on any tree" (Revelation 7:1).

Angels have a strong sense of right and wrong (2 Samuel 14:17), and rejoice whenever a sinner repents. However, they're also prepared to punish the wicked when necessary (Genesis 22:11; Exodus 14:19; Numbers 20:16; Psalms 34:7).

Angels carry the souls of the just to heaven and are always present when people pray. They work ceaselessly for God and will be present at His second coming, according to the Christian tradition.

GUARDIAN ANGELS

For thousands of years, people have gained comfort from knowing they had a wise, loving, protective guardian angel who looked after them from the moment they were born. Some people believe that guardian angels start looking after their charges from the moment of conception. I like the old story that says that the guardian angel appears when the baby laughs for the first time. It seems that our guardian angels have looked after us through many lifetimes, as well as in the periods between incarnations.

The concept of guardian angels began in ancient Mesopotamia, where people believed they had personal gods. They were known as *massar sulmi* ("the guardian of man's welfare"). The Zoroastrians called these protective beings *fravashis* or *arda fravash* (meaning "Holy Guardian Angels"). The fravashis originally guarded the borders of heaven but volunteer to come to earth to help individuals. The fravashi is also an ideal that the soul has to try to attain, and ultimately become one with after the person has died (Dhalla, 375–378). Similarly, the Assyrians and Babylonians had *keribu*, spirit guardians who protected the gates of temples and palaces.

The ancient Greeks had spirits called *daimons* who guided them through life. Plato believed that even before conception, a soul chose its future incarnation and a daimon to act as a teacher, guide, and supporter. In his book *The Republic*, Plato retells the ancient story of the three Fates, the Moirai or Moirae. Also known as daughters of the night, the Moirae supervise the process: Clotho (the spinner) spins the thread of a person's life on to a spindle, Lachesis (allotter, or a drawer of lots) then measures the thread with her measuring rod, and Atropos (meaning "unturnable," a metaphor for death) cuts the thread. Their process reveals the quality and length of life a soul will have in its upcoming incarnation. It also ensures that everyone fulfills the destiny assigned to them by the laws of the universe. Only Zeus, the god of fate, was able to step in and alter someone's fate. When people were born, they forgot all that had happened before birth and had to relearn the choices their souls had made. This is similar to the philosophy

I learned in a poem at high school: *Intimations of Immortality*, by the English poet William Wordsworth (1770–1850):

> Our birth is but a sleep and a forgetting:
> The Soul that rises with us, our life's Star,
> Hath had elsewhere its setting
> And cometh from afar:
> Not in entire forgetfulness,
> And not in utter nakedness,
> But trailing clouds of glory do we come
> From God, who is our home.

SOCRATES

The ancient Greek poet Hesiod (fl. ca. 750 BCE) was probably the first person to write about the concept of a daimon as a person's protecting spirit and lifelong companion (Parisen, 177). Three hundred years later, most ancient Greeks believed in daimones, supernatural beings that belonged between the gods and human beings. They believed that everyone had a daimon who guided them and determined their path through life. The philosopher Heraclitus of Ephesus (ca. 535–475 BCE) wrote: *Ethos anthropoi daimon*, which means "a person's character is [their] fate."

Another Greek philosopher, Socrates (470–399 BCE), was the first person to talk openly about his guardian angel. He called it a *daimonion*, which means (at least according to Cicero) "divine something." Socrates reported that his daimon regularly spoke to him, and, as he said himself in Plato's *Apology*, "always forbids me to do something which I am going to do, but never commands me to do anything." The daimonion started talking to Socrates when he was a child and constantly questioned everything.

There are many stories about Socrates and his daimon. One day while walking through the streets of Athens with a group of friends, Socrates stopped walking because his daimon told him not to take the particular route they were walking on. His friends ignored the advice of Socrates's daimon and continued walking. Suddenly and unexpectedly, they were run over by a herd of pigs.

Socrates had many enemies who accused him of corrupting the young. He was found guilty of the trumped-up charges and sentenced to die by taking poison. On the last day of his life, Socrates spoke to his friends about the soul and how it was everlasting and immortal. He convinced his friends of this notion, and according to Plato, drank the hemlock "rejoicing," as his soul was going to be free from the chains of the body.

The ancient Romans believed that every woman had a guardian spirit called a *juno* and every man had a *genius*. These were thought to be a higher power that created and maintained life. Like the Greek daimones, the juno and genius were present at the birth of their charges, determined their character, and tried to influence them to lead upright, honest lives. They accompanied them throughout life as tutelary spirits and watched over their descendants after their death.

Over time, Zoroastrian angelology was co-opted by Judaism to eventually become part of the Christian and Islamic belief systems as well. Belief in personal guardian angels goes back thousands of years (Jubilees 35:17, Testament of Levi 5:3, Philo De Gigantibus 12).

The first mention of a guardian angel in the Bible occurred when Yahweh told Moses: "Behold, I send an angel before thee, to keep thee in the way, and to bring thee into the place which I have prepared" (Exodus 23:20).

David the psalmist wrote that God "will give his angels charge of you, to guard you in all your ways" (Psalms 91:11). Jesus referred to guardian angels of children when he said, "Take heed that ye despise not one of these little ones; for I say unto you, That in heaven their angels do always behold the face of my Father which is in heaven" (Matthew 18:10).

After Peter was freed from prison by the Angel of the Lord, he went to the house of Mary, the mother of John. When he knocked on the door, a young servant came to open it. She heard his voice, and, instead of letting him in, she ran to tell a group of people what she had heard. They said, "Thou art mad. But she constantly affirmed that it was even so. Then said they, it is his angel" (Acts 12:15). St. Paul wrote in The Epistle to the Hebrews: "Are they [angels] not all ministering spirits, sent forth to minister for them who shall be heirs of salvation?" (Hebrews 1:14).

Guardian angels were first mentioned in noncanonical scripture in the book of Jubilees, which was written about 160–150 BCE: "And fear thou not on account of Jacob; for the guardian of Jacob is great and powerful and honoured, and praised more than the guardian of Esau" (35:17), (Charles, 1913).

The Greek playwright Menander of Athens (ca. 342–ca. 290 BCE), wrote: "Beside each man who's born on Earth, a guardian angel takes his stand to guide him through life's mysteries" (Adam, 60).

The early Church fathers believed in guardian angels, though they argued about whether heathens or people who had not been baptized had them. Saint Jerome wrote, "How great the dignity of the soul, since each one has from his birth an angel commissioned to guard it" (The Fathers of the Church, vol. 117). St. Basil (329–379) and St. John Chrysostom (ca. 347–420) thought that guardian angels appeared only after someone had been baptized

(St. Basil: Homily on Psalm 43; St. John Chrysostom: Homily 3 on Colossians). St. Jerome (ca. 340–420) thought that everyone had a guardian angel. Origen (ca. 184–ca. 253), arguably the greatest of the early Church fathers, went further than most, warning that people could have their guardian angels taken away from them if they were unworthy, especially if they were "unbelievers." He also wrote that people should pay attention to any admonitions from their guardian angels (Origen, 296). After much debate, eventually the Church fathers decided that everyone must have a guardian angel, as they were necessary to encourage people to become Christians.

Arguably the most influential person in the history of angelology is the author who claimed to be Dionysius the Areopagite. Commonly known as Pseudo-Dionysius, he may have been a late fifth-century Syrian monk. His true identity is unknown; it's assumed he adopted the name "Dionysius the Areopagite" to add credibility to his writing. The real Dionysius lived hundreds of years before the author who claimed his name and was briefly mentioned in the Bible (Acts 17:34). He was an early Greek convert to Christianity and became the first Bishop of Athens.

Pseudo-Dionysius's book, *The Celestial Hierarchy*, popularized the concept of nine choirs of angels, a belief many people still hold today. His writings had a major influence on Christian thought for almost fifteen hundred years. Most of Pseudo-Dionysius's ideas came from Neoplatonist philosophy, which was popular in the third century CE. The concept that angels mediated between God and humanity is an example. The Neoplatonists called the beings that communicated between God and humanity "daimons." When Pseudo-Dionysius Christianized their ideas, they became "angels."

About eight hundred years later, St. Bonaventure (1221–1274) wrote that guardian angels were affectionate and enjoyed socializing with other angels. They were a model for how human behavior should be, as there was no jealousy between different hierarchies of angels. He also speculated that guardian angels would feel upset and become distressed if their charges did not enter heaven.

Theologians continued to discuss the possibility that guardian angels could affect people's free will by telling them what to believe. St. Thomas Aquinas (1225–1274) responded to this by writing that guardian angels could act upon people's senses and imagination but not directly upon people's will (St. Thomas Aquinas, *Summa Theologica*, 1.3:3–4, 1:106:2, 1.111:2, and 1.108:7). Known at the time as the Angelic Doctor, St. Thomas believed that guardian angels could leave their charges temporarily but would never leave them permanently, no matter what sins the person had done. He also believed that guardian angels stayed with their charges after death and stood beside them in heaven.

Owing to the popularity of guardian angels at this time in history, a chapel dedicated to them was included in plans for Winchester Cathedral. The ceiling of this chapel was painted in 1241 and contains twenty angels who look down on the congregation through round windows similar to portholes. This beautiful chapel was (and is) a perfect place for people to pray with their guardian angels.

In 1608, Pope Paul V proclaimed that an annual feast day for the Holy Guardian Angels would be celebrated on October 2 each year.

In 1968, Pope Paul VI (1897–1978) sanctioned the establishment of the *Opus Sanctorum Angelorum*, or "the Work of the Holy Angels." Commonly known as Opus or Opus Angelorum, one of the aims of this organization is to encourage belief in guardian angels. Initiates of this organization progress through three stages.

The first stage lasts one year. During this time, initiates learn the names of their guardian angels and promise God that they will love their guardian angels and will act on their wishes. In the second stage, initiates take part in a candlelit ceremony and promise to become like angels and to venerate angels. The final stage includes a ceremony of consecration to the entire angelic hierarchy.

Guardian angels play a major role in Islam, too. They are considered to be celestial beings made of light who live in a mystical world. The Koran states: "He (God) sets guardians over you. At length, when death approaches one of you, Our angels take his soul, and they never fail in their duty" (Surah 6:61). In Islam, every person has four angels, known as *hafaza*. Two angels sit on the person's shoulders and provide protection during the day, and the other two perform the same task at night. The hafaza record every act, good and bad, that their charges think, say, and do.

In Hinduism, every living plant, animal, and person has a guardian spirit known as a *deva*, a Sanskrit word that translates to "shining one." These spiritual beings protect and look after their charges.

Judaism has included angels in its belief system since the Second Temple period (ca. 515 BCE–70 CE). In medieval times, according to the Pesikta Rabbati 44:1, a rabbinic interpretation of the Bible, Jews did believe in guardian angels (https://www.sefaria .org/Pesikta_Rabbati.44.1?lang=bi&with=all&lang2=en). In fact, the Talmud says that every Jew has eleven thousand guardian angels, and "every blade of grass has over it an angel saying 'grow.'" However, the popular idea of a personal guardian angel is not part of modern-day Judaism. Instead, every time someone performs a mitzvah (a good deed), they create an angel that provides protection. After the person dies, these angels testify on the person's behalf in heaven.

JOSEPH AND THE CERTAIN MAN

Many people know the story of Joseph and his cloak of many colors. Less familiar is the possibility that Joseph met his guardian angel.

When Joseph was seventeen years old, his father made him a multi-colored cloak. This infuriated Joseph's brothers, who knew that, as "he was the son of his old age" (Genesis 37:3), he was their father's favorite. Joseph had also been foolish enough to tell his brothers about a dream he'd had in which the brothers were binding sheaves in a field. In the dream, his brothers' sheaves made obeisance to his sheaf. This made his brothers extremely angry. Another dream angered them even more. One day, Joseph's father sent him to find his brothers to see how they were getting on with feeding their flocks.

Joseph set off, but made little progress until "a certain man found him" wandering in the fields (Genesis 37:15). This man told him that he'd overheard Joseph's brothers say they were going to Dothan. Joseph headed in that direction, and eventually found them. When his brothers saw him in the distance, they decided to kill him. However, they changed their minds, and sold him to slave traders who were on their way to Egypt. There, Joseph's dreams proved extremely useful to the Pharaoh.

This story is crucial to the history of Judaism. If the "certain man" hadn't told Joseph where to find his brothers, he wouldn't have been sold into slavery, but neither would there have been an Exodus, Moses would not have received the ten commandments, and most of the history of the Jewish people would never have occurred. Because of this, many centuries later, Jewish rabbis decided that the "certain man" must have been Joseph's guardian angel appearing in human form to make sure that Joseph's destiny unfolded in the way it should.

The concept of a guardian angel, personal spirit, or daimon can be found all around the world. Many people in West Africa, particularly in Benin and Nigeria, have a personal spirit known as *ehi*. The ehi stays with the person they're protecting during the day, but returns to Osa, their supreme deity, at night. The Sea Dayaks of Borneo have a *nyarong*, or spirit helper, who appears in people's dreams. The ancient Mayans had a *nahual*, an animal spirit, who guided people through life, especially through dreams and visions.

There are many beliefs and stories about guardian angels. Many people believe that we all have one guardian angel who looks after us throughout this lifetime. Probably as many believe that we have two guardian angels. Some early authorities, including Hermas and Gregory of Nyssa (330–395), believed that everyone was assigned both a good and an evil guardian angel. Others believe that we have an unlimited number of guardian angels who are prepared and willing to help us whenever we need them. The Talmud says that every Jew has 11,000 guardian angels (Davidson, 128). Some people believe that our guardian angel looks after us through all our incarnations, as well as during the time we spend between different lifetimes. Many believe that we have one guardian angel, but other angels are willing to step in and help us when we need them. The French theologian Peter Lombard (1100–1160) believed that guardian angels watched over several people at a time (Lombard, 2:11). Some people believe that angels are the spiritual aspect of ourselves and information comes to us through our superconscious mind directly connected to the Divine. As angels can appear in so many different shapes and forms, it seems that angels are what we believe them to be.

Tobias and Raphael

Archangel Raphael is considered the prince of the guardian angels, as he looks after all of humanity. Part of the reason for his reputation is due to the fact that he was Tobias' guardian angel in the book of Tobit, one of the books in the Apocrypha. This story tells us that we're never alone and always accompanied by an angel guardian who acts as a healing force to enable us to be the very best that we can be. The story of Tobit also enhanced Raphael's reputation as a healer and as one who looks after pilgrims and other travelers.

Tobit was a good, pious Jew, who was exiled in Nineveh about eight hundred years before the birth of Christ. The Jewish people were being held captive in Nineveh and King Sennacherib refused to let them bury their dead. Tobit and a small group of other men defied this edict and secretly buried the corpses.

One evening, Tobit was enjoying his dinner when he heard of another body that needed to be buried. He immediately abandoned his meal and left to bury the body. As he had been defiled from handling the body, he didn't return to his home but instead slept by the wall of a courtyard.

During the night, the droppings of sparrows who were resting on the wall fell into his eyes, and when he woke up, he was completely blind. He saw many physicians, but none were able to help him regain his sight. His wife, Anna, had to go out to work to help the family survive.

Tobit was fifty years old when this happened. Eight years later, Tobit was suicidal and prayed to God, pleading with him to let him die. He began getting his affairs in order, and asked Tobias, his only son, to travel to Media to collect some money he was owed by a business associate there. He told Tobias to find someone to travel with him for safety, and said he would pay the man for his time and work.

While this was happening in Nineveh, a woman in Media named Sarah was also suffering. She had been possessed by a demon called Asmodeus who had killed all seven of her husbands before any of the marriages had been consummated. Her parents thought that she would never find a husband, and her father, Raguel, prayed to God for help.

When God heard Tobit's and Raguel's prayers, he sent Raphael down to earth to restore Tobit's sight and to exorcise the demon from Sarah.

Tobias found a man called Azarias to travel with him. Azarias told Tobit that they were distant relatives. Unbeknownst to Tobias, Azarias was actually Raphael in human form.

Tobias and Azarias set off on their journey to Media. That evening, when Tobias was bathing in the Tigris River, a huge fish attacked him. Azarias told him to catch the fish, which he managed to do. When the fish was on the bank, Azarias told him to cut out the fish's heart, liver, and gall. They cooked and ate the rest of the fish.

When Tobias asked Azarias why they had saved the heart, liver, and gall, he was told that a smoke made from the heart and liver would exorcise evil spirits, and the gall would restore the sight of a man with a white film in his eyes.

The following morning, they resumed their journey. When they got close to Media, Azarias told Tobias that they should stay in the house of Raguel and that he should marry Sarah, Raguel's daughter.

Tobias became concerned when Azarias told him that all seven of her previous husbands had died on their wedding nights. Azarias managed to reassure him by telling him that on his wedding night, he should place some of the heart and liver from the fish on incense to create smoke. As soon as the demon smelled the smoke, he would leave Sarah, and never return.

Tobias agreed to marry Sarah, and everything happened as Azarias had predicted. Asmodeus, the demon, fled as soon as he smelled the smoke, and was "banished to the upmost parts of Egypt," where Raphael bound him with rope. During the night, Sarah's father dug a grave for Tobias, as he was convinced that he would not survive the night. In the morning, when he discovered that Tobias was still alive, he ordered his servants to fill up the grave before Tobias saw it. The wedding celebrations lasted for fourteen days, and during that time Azarias collected the money that was owed to Tobit.

Once the celebrations were over, Tobias took his bride, Sarah, and Azarias back home to Nineveh. Tobias anointed his father's eyes with the gall of the fish, and Tobit's sight was miraculously restored. The grateful family offered Azarias half of the money that Tobias had brought back from Media.

Azarias then told Tobit and Tobias that he had brought Tobit's prayers, Sarah's prayers, and Tobit's good deeds to God, and that God had sent him to heal Tobit and Sarah. Azarias finished by saying: "I am Raphael, one of the seven holy angels, which present the prayers of the saints, and go in before the Glory of the Holy One" (Tobit 12:15). When Tobit and Tobias heard these words, they fell to the ground in fear, but Raphael told them not to be afraid. He told them to lead good, righteous lives, to praise God, and to write down everything that had happened.

YOUR GUARDIAN ANGEL

Your guardian angel is your spiritual friend and mentor who watches over you, and unceasingly tries to guide and protect you. Your guardian angel can't eliminate any karmic factors you'll encounter in this lifetime. However, they will do everything possible to ensure that the karmic effects are dealt with in a positive and creative manner to help you progress in the future. You possess free will, and your angel will never overrule this. Neither will your angel help you if you choose to ignore their advice. Conversely, your angel will always assist you if you're willing to accept help. The biggest problem most guardian angels have is that the person they're looking after is completely unaware of their existence.

No matter what you do, your guardian angel constantly surrounds you with unconditional love. Your guardian angel sees your divine perfection and wants to help you become the very best you that it's possible to be. They want you to be happy and fulfilled, and they constantly work on your behalf. Your salvation is your guardian angel's ultimate goal.

Your guardian angel will help you develop any character traits or skills that will make your progress in this lifetime smoother, happier, and richer. For instance, you might ask your angel for help in gaining confidence, peace of mind, patience, wisdom, trust, love, forgiveness, or acceptance. There is no limit to what you can ask for, and if it benefits you and your soul, your guardian angel will be more than willing to help you develop it.

Naturally, your guardian angel will also help you gain control over negative traits such as addiction, anger, jealousy, egotism, and dishonesty. However, you have to take the first step and ask your angel for the particular help you need.

Your guardian angel can also help you to contact other angels for specific purposes. If you need healing, for example, you could ask your guardian angel to speak to Archangel Raphael for you. Your guardian angel will also contact other people's guardian angels for you whenever necessary. If, for instance, you're having problems with someone, or need to discuss a delicate matter, you can ask your guardian angel to speak with that person's guardian angel, and resolve the situation. Pope Pius XI did this regularly.

POPE PIUS XI

Pope Pius XI (1857–1939) prayed to his guardian angel twice a day, in addition to whenever he was going to have a meeting with someone who might be difficult to deal with. In that situation, he asked his guardian angel to speak with the other person's guardian angel beforehand. He claimed that the two guardian angels quickly resolved any difficulties and the meetings would go well. He also advised that upon moving into a new neighborhood, you should ask your guardian angel to talk to the guardian angels of your new neighbors. Pope Pius said: "We have always seen ourselves as wonderfully helped by our guardian angel. Very often, we feel that he is here, close by, ready to help us" (Huber, 14).

A number of other popes have also talked about guardian angels. Pope Pius XII (1876–1958) said that when he stood in front of the crowds at St. Peter's Square, he saw all the people in addition to their guardian angels.

Your guardian angel is constantly watching over you and sends you messages that you may or may not pick up. For instance, you might hear a small, quiet voice talking to you. You could also feel a gentle, subtle touch on your arm or shoulder. You might see feathers, especially small white ones. If you find these in unlikely places, it's probably your guardian angel trying to get through to you. If a light happens to flicker for no apparent reason, it could be a sign from your angel. Other signs include a sense of warmth and comfort, a slight breeze with no apparent cause, beautiful scents, celestial music, flashes of light, and finding small denomination coins. You might receive messages from your guardian angels in your dreams. Whenever anything unusual happens, such as a coincidence, analyze it to see if it could be a message for you.

You could say that your guardian angel is your best friend, a perfect life coach, and, in a very real sense, your "other half."

Ideally, you should also be proactive, and let your guardian angel know that you want to develop a closer connection with them.

CHAPTER TWO
WHAT DOES YOUR GUARDIAN ANGEL DO?

Your guardian angel's main task is to protect, guide, and look after your mind, body, and soul in all of your lifetimes. In the Christian tradition, the main responsibility of a guardian angel is to encourage the soul to lead a good life, which will ensure it will ultimately get admitted into heaven. Many people believe that your guardian angel has helped you in all of your previous incarnations and will look after you in your future lifetimes as well. Consequently, your guardian angel will never abandon or leave you. Guardian angels are like mothers who are always watching their charges in the hope of seeing signs of improvement. St. Basil described guardian angels as our "shepherds" and as "guardians of the faithful."

Guardian angels have a number of important tasks. They provide us with spiritual and physical protection when the soul is in danger. This is usually to protect us from violence or mental attacks in the physical world, but guardian angels also provide protection from the "snare of the devil" (2 Timothy 2:26).

They encourage good thoughts and deeds. The soul is seldom aware that its guardian angel is gently inspiring the person to think kind thoughts and do the right thing. Occasionally, this influence will be noticed in the form of an intuition or thought. It may be felt as the voice of conscience. On October 2, 2014, Pope Francis said that when we have a feeling such as "I should not do this; this is not right," be careful, as that voice belongs to our guardian angel, or "travelling companion" (http://www.catholicnewsagency.com/news/be-like-children-believe-in-your-guardian-angel-pope-says-55343/). It's important to note that your guardian angel can help you only if you're willing to listen and take advice. Your guardian angel will never interfere with your free will, but they will let you know when you have sinned.

Guardian angels pray with their charges. A popular belief is that guardian angels interweave their prayers with those of their souls to make the prayers more effective and more pleasing to the Divine.

Guardian angels correct people's souls when they have strayed. If someone has succumbed to evil and negativity, their guardian angel will do everything possible to encourage the person to return to the path of righteousness. Guardian angels celebrate when their charges make spiritual progress. They also mourn when their charges succumb to negativity and temptation.

In the Christian tradition, guardian angels reveal the will of God. A good example of this is recorded in Genesis 22:9–18, where an angel prevented Abraham from sacrificing Isaac and told him of the huge influence his descendants would have on the world: "And in thy seed shall all the nations of the earth be blessed; because thou hast obeyed my voice" (Genesis 2:18).

Guardian angels provide signs to lead us where we're meant to go. They are willing to protect or help anyone their person names. All that's required is to name the person and ask your angel to provide whatever help and comfort is necessary.

Guardian angels provide comfort and inner strength to people when they are suffering.

Guardian angels provide guidance and help their charges make good moral decisions. Whenever people are tempted to make the wrong choice, their guardian angels will do everything they can to encourage their charges to make the right decision. Many years ago, I gave a series of talks at a maximum-security prison, and several prisoners told me that they had heard a still, quiet voice telling them not to do something, but they'd done it anyway. If they'd spent a few moments listening to their guardian angels, they would have been enjoying life in freedom with their family and friends, rather than wasting years of their lives in prison.

Guardian angels physically help people. In his book *The Dialogue on Miracles*, the Cistercian monk Caesarius of Heisterbach (1180–1240) tells a story about a young woman who was physically supported by her angel while she was being hanged. When the rope was eventually cut, the angel gently lowered her to the ground (Caesarius, 1929). There are many modern-day accounts of guardian angels who have temporarily manifested as human beings to help their charges in times of danger. There's an often-told story about a farmer's wife named Edith in the early twentieth century who was home alone when a stranger knocked at her door. He asked her if she was by herself. She said her husband was home, and called out his name. Much to her surprise, a voice that sounded exactly like her husband's answered her from upstairs, and the stranger left as quickly as he could (http://www .opusangelorum.org/). There are three possibilities as to what created the voice. Could it have been Edith's guardian angel protecting her? Might it perhaps have been her husband's guardian angel? Or could it have been the stranger's guardian angel, successfully preventing him from committing a crime? St. John Bosco and his guardian angel who appeared as a dog, when necessary, is another good example of a guardian angel who provided physical protection.

St. John Bosco and Grigio

The story of St. John Bosco (1815–1888), a priest who worked with homeless boys in the slums of Turin, is a fascinating one for many reasons, including the fact that his guardian angel appeared numerous times in the form of a huge wolf-like dog who never ate, drank, or grew old. Many of the boys John Bosco tried to work with weren't interested in being helped or saved, and he was constantly in danger of being beaten up and robbed. One evening, in 1852, he walked through a dangerous part of Turin while praying to God to help him. He suddenly noticed a large, gray dog was following him. The dog was so huge, John thought it might be a wolf. He spoke to the dog, who immediately approached and walked beside him. The dog was friendly, and John decided to call him *Grigio* (pronounced *gree-jo*), the word for "gray" in Italian. The dog accompanied John all the way home, and then left.

A few days later, when John was walking through another dangerous part of town, Grigio mysteriously appeared and stayed at John's side until he returned home. This became a regular occurrence. Whenever John was walking by himself in the slums, Grigio would appear and stay with him until he got home safely.

On one occasion, someone fired two shots at John. The shots missed, and the shooter tried to wrestle John to the ground. Grigio appeared and chased the man away. On another occasion, two men pulled a sack over the priest's head. While discussing what they'd do next, John heard Grigio growling at the men as he chased them away. Shortly after this, John was ambushed and surrounded by several men armed with large sticks. Again, Grigio arrived and chased the men away.

Grigio occasionally spent time in John's home and enjoyed playing with the younger boys who lived there. When necessary, he prevented John from leaving the house by lying down in front of the gate to block the exit. The first time this happened, a neighbor arrived shortly afterward to tell John that a group of dangerous men were waiting for him.

Grigio stayed with John for more than thirty years while he continued his work. He started his first school in 1845, and the society he established was approved by Pope Pius IX in 1879. This society still exists today and is called the Salesians of St. John Bosco.

The quote St. John Bosco is best known for is: "When tempted, invoke your angel. He is more eager to help you than you are to be helped! Ignore the devil and do not be afraid of him: he trembles and flees at your guardian angel's sight" (Bruno, part 4).

There's an intriguing footnote to this story. In 1959, Pope John XXIII had St. John Bosco's casket and remains brought to Rome to be venerated. On the return trip to Turin, the Salesians stopped at La Spezia to wait for the casket, which was being transported in a van. While they were waiting, a large gray dog, looking much like a wolf, joined them. One of the brothers used a stick to chase the dog away. However, the dog returned and approached another brother who liked dogs. This man patted him and made a fuss of him. The van finally arrived, and the dog accompanied the casket, even following it into a church, where he lay down under the casket and refused to move.

The brothers started joking that the dog might be Grigio and let him remain there throughout the viewing. The dog growled when anyone not associated with the official party got near to the casket, but was happy when the brothers allowed babies to touch it.

When the viewing ended, the dog played with the younger brothers and a group of schoolboys. He went to lunch with the brothers but sat in a corner and refused to eat anything. After lunch, he disappeared and was found inside the church guarding the casket. This should have been impossible, as the church had been locked.

The dog followed the casket back to the van, and when it drove off, he followed it for a while and then disappeared. You can find photographs of this dog online: https://dogs-in-history.blogspot .com/2018/04/grigio-father-boscos-guardian-angel.html.

Guardian angels can guide us to people who can help us. Many people owe their success to a chance meeting with someone who changed the course of their lives for the better. My father was going to become a carpenter and follow in his father's footsteps. When he was twelve years old, his parents had a boarder for a few months. This man told my father that with his brain and humanitarian qualities, he should become a doctor. My father ultimately became a surgeon and was able to fulfill the role he was born to do. Our guardian angels enable these apparently chance encounters to occur.

Guardian angels protect and help souls at the moment of death. In the Catholic tradition, guardian angels visit and care for their charges if they're sent to purgatory. Once these souls have been purified of all their sins, their guardian angels accompany them to heaven. Mary, Queen of the Angels, decides when the souls are ready. Other traditions believe that guardian angels continue to look after the souls of their charges after they've died. Many people believe that they are looked after by the same guardian angel in all their incarnations, not just the current life.

Guardian angels can make themselves known to their charges, even if they have shown no previous interest in them. This normally happens when the person needs help of some sort, but may not be aware of it. A well-documented example of this occurred when a guardian angel told a woman, known as AB in her doctor's notes, to seek medical help for an illness.

AB

In 1984, a forty-year-old woman, living with her family in London, was at home reading when she heard a voice inside her head. The voice started by saying, "Please don't be afraid," and then told her that "it" and a friend wanted to help her. It gave her three pieces of information she didn't know and told her to check them out. The woman investigated and confirmed that the information was true. However, she was concerned that she had "gone mad," as she had never experienced voices in her head before. She went to see her doctor, who referred her to Dr. I. O. Azuonye, a consultant psychiatrist.

Dr. Azuonye diagnosed a hallucinatory psychosis and prescribed counseling and medication. After two weeks, the voice in her head stopped and she traveled overseas on vacation to celebrate her return to sanity. While she was away, the voice returned, telling her that she had to return home immediately, as she needed immediate treatment for an illness. When she got back home to London, the voice gave her an address to visit. Mainly to reassure her, her husband drove her there, and they found the address was for the computerized tomography department of a large hospital. The voice then told her to go in and request a brain scan because she had a tumor in her brain and her brain stem was inflamed.

Dr. Azuonye requested a brain scan purely to reassure the woman, who was extremely distressed because the voices had given her correct information in the past; she was convinced she had a tumor. The request was turned down, as such an expensive investigation could not be justified: the woman, whom Dr. Azuonye called AB in his notes, had no symptoms. Despite criticism from his colleagues, Dr. Azuonye persisted and AB finally had a brain scan, followed by another one a month later. The scans indicated a brain tumor that was successfully removed.

When AB recovered consciousness after the operation, the voices said, "We are pleased to have helped you. Goodbye." AB made a full recovery and phoned Dr. Azuonye twelve years later to wish him Happy Christmas and to let him know that she had kept excellent health since the operation.

In an article he wrote for the *British Medical Journal*, Dr. Azuonye confirmed that this was the only instance he had ever encountered in which hallucinatory voices expressed interest in someone's well-being, gave a specific diagnosis, recommended a particular hospital that specialized in the type of treatment needed, and then said farewell after a successful outcome had been achieved (https://www.ncbi.nlm.nih.gov/pmc/articles/PMC2128009/pdf/9448541.pdf).

There is no logical explanation for AB's experience. However, it may well be a case of AB's guardian angel stepping in and helping her at a time when she needed it.

Unfortunately, few people are aware of what their guardian angels are doing for them. St. Ignatius of Loyola (1491–1556), the founder of the Jesuits (Society of Jesus) said that people had to advance spiritually before they could feel and experience the faint and gentle yet insistent energy of their angels.

Saint Bonaventure (1221–1274), the Italian theologian and prolific author, was called "The Devout Teacher" and "The Seraphic Doctor." He was a hugely influential figure in the history of Western spirituality. In his *Commentaria* (https://franciscan-archive .org/bonaventura/sent.html), he listed twelve works of charity that guardian angels perform for their charges, as well as the quotations from the Bible and Apocrypha that enabled him to create his list:

1. Whenever necessary, guardian angels reprimand us for our faults. (Judges 2: 1–2)

2. Guardian angels release us from the bonds of our sins. (Acts 12: 7)

3. Guardian angels remove anything that impedes our progress in leading a good life. (Exodus 12:12)

4. Guardian angels constrain any demons who might be afflicting us. (Tobit 12: 3)

5. Guardian angels constantly try to teach us what we need to know. (Daniel 9: 22)

6. Guardian angels reveal secrets that we need to know. (Genesis 18:17)

7. Guardian angels provide consolation. (Tobit 5: 13)

8. Guardian angels comfort us on our way to the other side. (1 Kings 19: 7)

9. Guardian angels lead us back to God. (Tobit 5: 15)

10. Guardian angels defeat our enemies. (Isaiah 37: 36)

11. Guardian angels alleviate our temptations. (Genesis 32: 24)

12. Guardian angels pray for us and carry our prayers to God. (Tobit 12: 12)

In summary, your guardian angel works hard to protect you, guide you, and keep you safe. Your guardian angel is your companion, comforter, teacher, mentor, and friend.

WHY DOESN'T YOUR GUARDIAN ANGEL ALWAYS PROVIDE HELP?

If our guardian angels are always ready to help us, why don't they immediately step in and provide help and protection during times of danger or difficulty? This is a question that people have debated and thought about for thousands of years, and there is no definitive answer. Here are some reasons that might explain why this happens.

Karma

Karma is a philosophy that dates back at least three thousand years and appears in ancient Hindu texts known as the *Upanishads*. Karma is the law of cause and effect that says we ultimately reap what we sow. It has nothing to do with fate, as everyone has free will and consequently creates their own destiny. Karma is created by people's thoughts, words, actions, and intent. People who do good deeds will ultimately be rewarded for them. Likewise, people who commit bad deeds will ultimately have to pay the price to balance the books.

Guardian angels are unable to prevent their charges from meeting their karma as they progress through life. However, they can help the soul move in directions that will enable the karmic effects to be dealt with in creative and constructive ways, rather than in ways that might be damaging or destructive.

Tests

Another reason guardian angels don't always step in may be because the person is being tested and will hopefully emerge from the experience as a stronger, wiser, and more capable person.

We are all living in our present incarnations to learn whatever it is we need to learn to grow and evolve in knowledge and wisdom. If all we had to do was ask our guardian angel for help, knowing that it would always be provided, we wouldn't need to take the chances or risks that are essential to learn the life lessons we need.

Of course, we all make stupid and foolish decisions all the time. The fact that humans possess free will must be frustrating for guardian angels, who have to watch their charges doing things that will hinder their spiritual growth and development.

Keeping on Track

A person's guardian angel might be concerned that the person is veering away from the path they are supposed to be following in this incarnation. In this case, the guardian angel might wait until the person makes a mistake, and the loss or setback will hopefully encourage them to think about the situation and get back on track.

YOUR GUARDIAN ANGEL'S BIGGEST PROBLEM

The biggest problem facing guardian angels is that their charges are often unaware of their presence, and of their desire to help, encourage, and nurture. Everyone has a guardian angel, but it's possible that people need to believe in guardian angels before any communication can occur. In one of his boyhood conversations with his guardian angel, John C. Lilly asked: "Will you always take care of me?" The angel replied: "Yes, as long as you believe in me. Will you always believe in me?" (Lilly, 38).

DR. JOHN C. LILLY

Renowned American physician, neuroscientist, biologist, philosopher, and writer Dr. John Lilly (1915–2001) wrote in his autobiography that he saw his guardian angel for the first time when he was just three years old. He was about to punish his dog, Jamey, for biting him when he was about to fall over a wall and into a ravine, when a "being" appeared. He saw it as a radiant being who filled him with feelings of love and safety. The angel told him not to punish his dog, as he had sent him to pull John to safety (Lilly, 38).

While attending mass at the age of seven, he felt the church around him disappear to reveal God surrounded by choirs of angels. John himself was held up by two angels to allow the divine light to wash over him.

John contracted tuberculosis at the age of ten. While in a feverous state, a being came to him and asked him if he would like to go away with him. John replied that he wanted to continue to play with his friends and ultimately grow up. The being was happy with this answer, and told John that one day he would have to go away with him. John asked the being if he would stay with him, or go away. The being replied: "I will be with you always, as long as you believe you will be able to meet with me" (Lilly, 39).

These, and other childhood experiences involving what he called his "holy guardian angels," remained with him for the rest of his life.

Fortunately, guardian angels need only the slightest acknowledgment to step in and transform the lives of the people they're watching over. Your guardian angel can't help you unless you're willing to accept their help.

MEET YOUR GUARDIAN ANGEL

Your guardian angel wants to be close to you. During the course of your life, they will have sent you many signs that you may have failed to recognize. This is not unusual; many people live their entire lives without ever noticing the signals their guardian angels have sent. Angels often appear when people are undergoing stressful and difficult times in their lives. You are bound to have had your share of traumatic experiences but were so immersed in your problems that you failed to notice them.

I met my guardian angel when I was in my mid-twenties. My wife was pregnant when my business failed, and we had to sell our home and car. For a while, I worked three jobs to pay off debt. During the day I worked in a warehouse and had plenty of time to think about the situation we were in. It took me a long time to realize that much of our misfortune was my own making. If I'd made different decisions, the outcome would have been different, and I would still have been running my own business instead of doing menial work for other people. Once I accepted this, I also realized that I'd chosen to ignore the advice I'd been constantly given by a still, quiet voice inside my head. This voice had consistently given me good advice, but I'd paid no attention to it. At the time, I had no idea where that voice came from, and if I'd paid attention to it, I would have probably called it my conscience or inner mind. It took me quite a while to realize that it was my guardian angel.

You can call on angels whenever you wish. However, there are also times when your guardian angel is more likely to contact you. If you're happy and everything is going well with your life, the angels will probably leave you alone. However, they're likely to try to make contact:

1. If you start showing an interest in spiritual matters, and develop a deeper understanding of yourself and the universe.

2. If you start doing whatever you were placed here to do. Your guardian angel will be overjoyed when you discover your purpose in this incarnation.

3. If you've been through a traumatic experience, and are finally ready to start healing yourself.

4. If you feel vulnerable and lost, and need a reminder that you are here for a reason.

5. If you've taken the wrong path in life, and are ready to pursue the path you're meant to be on.

6. If you've become cynical about life, and need a gentle nudge to get you back on track.

Your guardian angel will let you know of their presence in many different ways. You could discover your angel in the way I did—become aware of a voice inside your head. You might, for instance, smell a beautiful scent, notice an orb or strange bright light, find a small coin, or feather, especially a white one, see recurring numbers, experience a sudden change in temperature, see butterflies nearby, or feel a tingling sensation on your skin, or at the top of your head in the area of your crown chakra. You might notice that your family pet is gazing intently at something you can't see. Similarly, a baby might smile at something outside the range of your vision. As your guardian angel knows you better than anyone else, your angel might use something that has a special or personal significance to you.

HOW TO EXPERIENCE YOUR GUARDIAN ANGEL

Many people expect their guardian angel to appear in front of them wearing flowing robes, displaying large wings, and holding a harp. That may happen occasionally, but it's unlikely. If you're ever fortunate enough to see an angel, the chances are they will look like an ordinary person, and you may not realize who it is until much later. Most people who communicate with angels experience them in a variety of ways, but few ever get to see them. The only time people see an angel is when the matter is important or urgent, and the Divine considers it necessary. However, even though most people never get to see an angel, everyone can learn to contact their guardian angel.

Here are nineteen effective ways you can use to contact your guardian angel.

A Sense of Knowing

You may gradually experience a sense of knowing that you are safe and protected, and realize that your guardian angel is constantly close at hand.

Over the years, many people have told me how they first became aware that their angel was constantly with them. One man I met experienced it when he was sent to a youth prison. He was terrified and cried himself to sleep on his first night there. He woke up in the middle of the night, suddenly knowing that he was safe and protected and that everything would work out in the end. He went back to sleep again and emerged from his cell the next morning feeling nervous but confident that he would survive the experience.

"I'd heard of all the terrible things that happen in those places," he told me, "But I never experienced any of it. The other guys left me alone. I think maybe they sensed that I was being helped. That experience on the worst day of my life turned my life around." He now works as a counselor and motivational speaker.

A good way to experience this sense of knowing is to sit down quietly in a comfortable chair, close your eyes, and relax. Start by inhaling deeply through your nose, hold the breath for a few seconds, and then exhale through your mouth. Do this twice more, and then forget about your breathing. Focus on your toes and allow them to relax. Follow this by relaxing your feet, and allow the relaxation to drift into your calf muscles, thigh muscles, and up into your abdomen, chest, shoulders, arms, hands, neck, and head.

Once you feel fully relaxed, focus on your breathing again, and enjoy the pleasant feelings of relaxation and peace you're experiencing. Your mind will drift away every now and again. This is natural. Whenever you become aware of it, dismiss the thought, and focus on your breathing again.

While doing this, you might feel your guardian angel's presence and realize that you are safe and protected. This could happen the first time you try this exercise, but is more likely to occur after several sessions. Once you've made contact this way, you'll be able to use it to communicate with your angel whenever you wish.

Create Your Own Sacred Space

No matter where you live, you can create your own sacred space where you can communicate with your guardian angel. If possible, find somewhere where you can communicate with your guardian angel without being disturbed or bothered by others. Your sacred space can be indoors or out. You may have a particular place inside your home that can be used solely for this purpose. If you're like most people, though, you might have to use a shelf, small table, or a corner of a desk to act as your altar. Ask your guardian angel to help you select a suitable place and to select anything you wish to place on it. You might start with a beautiful cloth and place on it anything you consider spiritual or makes you think of the angelic realms. You can decorate your altar with a few crystals, a candle or two, flowers, small ornaments, and anything else that has spiritual value to you.

Once you've created your special sacred space, you can do anything you wish inside it. You might talk to your guardian angel, pray, meditate, or write in a spiritual journal. You might want to do something physical, or sing or dance in front of it. These actions help infuse the area with your love and spiritual essence.

Use your sacred space regularly. During your prayers or meditations, speak to your guardian angel. You can do this silently or out loud. In time, this special place will become more and more spiritual. In some cases, this spirituality will even become apparent to others who have no idea that you are using the place to communicate with your guardian angel. Communicate with your guardian angel every time you're in this special place and remain alert for a reply.

You may be fortunate enough to see your guardian angel when you're in your sacred space. A good way to encourage this is to close your eyes and picture your guardian angel in your mind.

Your angel will appear in your imagination in the shape and form that you expect. Silently talk to your imaginary figure, telling it that you would love to see your guardian angel. Do this regularly, and (probably when you least expect it), you may get to meet your guardian angel.

Visit your altar every day to keep the spiritual energy alive. Replace the flowers regularly. Light the candle, burn some incense, play some music, and use the time you spend in front of your altar to deepen your relationship with your guardian angel.

Angelic Invocation of Protection

The word "invocation" is derived from the Latin *advoco*, which means "summon." An invocation is usually performed to summon a deity, angel, or spiritual power.

With this ritual you'll be able to surround yourself with angelic protection whenever you need it. I always perform this before performing any activities involving the angelic realms. If necessary, you can also perform a shortened version of it, by visualizing the four main archangels surrounding you with protection whenever you find yourself in a difficult situation.

You can perform the invocation anywhere you wish. I like to perform it outdoors, but sometimes weather and a desire for privacy force me indoors. Make sure that you won't be disturbed for at least half an hour.

The space you use will need to be at least eight feet square, as you're going to construct a magic circle that will be approximately six to eight feet in diameter. When I'm performing this invocation indoors, I use a circular rug to indicate the circle. When I'm working outdoors, I often mark out the circle with rope or cord or sometimes stones. Instead of creating a physical circle, I sometimes visualize the circle I'm working within. (If the ritual you're going to be performing inside the circle is lengthy or requires items, such as candles and other items, place a table and a straight-backed chair in the middle of the circle. You should be facing east when you sit down in the chair.)

If you have time, enjoy a leisurely bath before the invocation, and put on clean, loose-fitting clothes. This has the effect of separating the invocation from your normal, everyday life. The bath also gives you time to think about the invocation while you're relaxing in the warm water.

You've constructed the circle, bathed, and put on clean clothes. You're now ready to start the invocation.

Stand outside the circle, and smile as you're about to summon the four great archangels: Raphael, Michael, Gabriel, and Uriel. Take a deep breath, and step into the circle as you exhale. Move to the center and face east.

Close your eyes, and visualize Archangel Raphael standing in front of you. It makes no difference how you "see" Archangel Raphael. You might visualize him as a large, powerful angel with huge wings. You might see him as a traveler with a staff, water gourd, and large fish. You might see him as a swirling ball of color, or maybe feel his presence in your mind. Whatever image or impression comes into your mind will be the right one for you. When you feel Raphael is in front of you, start talking. I prefer to speak out loud, but you might prefer to talk to him in your mind, especially if there are people in the next room. What you say is entirely up to you. You might say something along the lines of: "Thank you, Archangel Raphael, for your support and protection. I'm grateful to you for being here for me, and for your guidance and healing. Thank you."

With your eyes still closed, turn ninety degrees to face south. Visualize Archangel Michael in your mind. I visualize Michael as a tall man wearing chain mail, wielding a sword in one hand and with one foot resting on a dragon. He holds a set of scales in his free hand. This is a composite of the many paintings I've seen of Archangel Michael over the years. Your image of Michael may be completely different. Whatever you see will be right for you. Once you sense Michael's presence, speak to him. You might say: "Thank you, Archangel Michael, for your support and protection. Thank you for giving me courage and strength when I most need it. I am very grateful for everything you do to help me. Thank you."

Turn another ninety degrees to face west. Visualize Archangel Gabriel as clearly as you can. I "see" Gabriel as a tall man wearing green and blue robes. He holds a lily in one hand to symbolize the purity of the Virgin Mary. He carries a trumpet in his other hand, and will use it to wake the dead on Judgment Day. Again, this is a composite of different pictures I've seen of Archangel Gabriel over the years; your picture of Gabriel might be completely different from mine. Speak to Gabriel when you sense his presence. You might say: "Thank you, Archangel Gabriel, for your gentleness and devotion. Thank you for being God's messenger and for all your help and support. I am very grateful. Thank you."

Turn to face north. This time, visualize Archangel Uriel standing in front of you. I see Uriel as a powerful-looking man with dark, curly hair and a brown beard. He carries a scroll in one hand. On the palm of his other hand is a burning flame. Most paintings of Uriel show this flame, as he is known as the "flame of God." Naturally, your image of Uriel may be quite different to mine. Again, once you sense his presence, say something along the lines of: "Thank you, Archangel Uriel, for all your help and support. Thank you for giving me fresh insights and ideas. Thank you for forcing me to make changes when I'm reluctant to do them myself. Thank you."

Turn to face Archangel Raphael again. You are now totally surrounded and protected by the four great archangels. Inside this circle of protection, you can conduct any rituals that you wish knowing that you are safe, secure, and loved. At this point, you can open your eyes, depending on what you're going to do during the ritual. After you've gained experience with this invocation, you'll find yourself able to perform all of it with your eyes open and to "see" the great archangels just as clearly as you did with your eyes closed.

When the ritual you're performing is over, face Archangel Raphael again and thank him for his love, help, and protection. Say goodbye and visualize him fading from view. Repeat with Archangels Michael, Gabriel, and Uriel.

Once the invocation is over, you can step outside the circle. As soon as you can, eat and drink something to help you become fully grounded again. I eat nuts and raisins and drink water. I may follow that with something alcoholic, but it depends on the time of day I perform the ritual and what I intend to do afterwards.

This invocation provides you with protection while you're performing spiritual work. You can also use it whenever you need protection. If you have a minute or two to prepare, you can visualize yourself surrounded by the four great archangels surrounding you with love and protection. If you have only a few moments, you should say: "Raphael, Michael, Gabriel, and Uriel, please protect me." Finally, if you need help and protection urgently, call out to Archangel Michael, God's warrior angel. Say: "Michael! I need your help now!" I've had to do that on three occasions, and Archangel Michael was there instantly each time to provide me with help.

Dreams

We all dream—people who say they don't simply fail to remember them. Dreams help us evaluate and sort out what is happening in our lives so we can function effectively when we're awake. It's common to experience your guardian angel in your dreams, especially if you tell yourself when you're lying in bed waiting for sleep that you'll dream of your guardian angel and will remember the dream when you wake up. Repeat this as often as necessary until you remember a dream of your angel. I find it helps if I have a particular question I want to ask. I use who, what, where, when, why and how questions, and repeat them three to five times before falling asleep. If you don't have a question, tell your guardian angel that you need guidance to help you keep on track to fulfill your soul's purpose.

Be patient. You may not receive or remember anything when you first try this. However, continue practicing and eventually you'll start to remember your dreams. It's also possible to not receive a complete answer in a single dream. Rest assured that over time, you'll learn all that you need to know.

You can't do this when you're woken by an alarm clock or a sudden loud noise, but there is a good way to recall your dreams when you wake up naturally. If you wake up with a memory of part of a dream, lie as still as you can, and see if you can recall the entire dream. Change position or get up *only* after you've recaptured as much information as you can.

Keep a pen and paper or some other form of recording device beside your bed so you can write down everything you remember before the dream fades. Sometimes you may not remember your dreams but will have an answer to your question. You should always record these to make sure you don't forget them, and it's a good idea to keep a dream diary to gradually build up a valuable record of everything your subconscious mind is working on.

Repetitive dreams are often a sign of angelic communication. If you're not sure what the dream means, ask your guardian angel to send you a dream that will clarify it for you.

Thoughts and Feelings

Everyone experiences thoughts and feelings all day, every day. Every now and again, though, we instinctively know that a particular thought or feeling came from another source rather than from our subconscious minds. Many creative people experience this on a regular basis. I believe thoughts and feelings of this sort come from our guardian angels.

Usually I experience these thoughts as if someone an inch away from my ear is whispering to me. A good friend of mine hears these thoughts as if he's quietly talking to himself inside his head. Another friend experiences a sense of warmness in his body and uses these sensations and messages to help him in his business. He told me, "These messages tell me I'm on the right track. If I follow the feeling, I'll make the right decision. If I ignore it, I always regret it later on."

The technical term for experiences of this sort is clairaudience, which means "clear hearing." It describes the ability to receive psychic impressions of sounds and voices that are not heard by others. Joan of Arc (ca. 1412–1431) is a good example of someone who used clairaudience. She started hearing voices at the age of thirteen and used this skill to communicate with Saint Margaret, Saint Catherine, and Archangel Michael. George Frideric Handel (1685–1759) believed angels helped him compose the "Hallelujah" chorus in the *Messiah*.

Thoughts and intuitions are the "still, small voice" that spoke to Elijah on Mount Sinai (1 Kings 19:12). As the voice is quiet and gentle, it's easily overlooked.

Clairsentience means "clear feeling" and is the ability to feel your guardian angel's presence. It means that you're sensitive to what's going on around you. Most people who communicate regularly with their guardian angel develop this ability. If you're empathetic and good at picking up other people's emotional states, you already possess this quality.

Intuition

We all experience intuitive hunches every now and again, usually closely related to our thoughts and feelings. A quote frequently attributed to Albert Einstein says: "The only real valuable thing is intuition." Intuition is a sense of knowing without using thought. An intuitive flash or insight bypasses the logical brain and gives us the answer instantly. Parapsychologists call this phenomenon claircognizance, "clear knowing." It describes the ability to know something (usually about the future) without knowing how or why you know.

Researchers have demonstrated that we can receive and act on these hunches without necessarily being consciously aware of them. William E. Cox, a parapsychologist, conducted an experiment using passengers who traveled on certain trains. He wanted to compare the number of passengers on trains that were involved in accidents to the number of people on trains that arrived safely to their destinations. He used the number of passengers traveling on a particular route, seven, fourteen, twenty-one, and twenty-eight days before the same train was involved in an accident. Although they didn't do it knowingly, many passengers somehow managed to avoid the accident-bound trains. They might have slept in, decided to have a day off work, or simply missed the train. In eleven train accidents, seven carried fewer passengers than they had on the previous day. Six carried fewer passengers than they had one week earlier, and four of them transported fewer passengers on the day of the accident than they had on any of the previous eight days. William Cox extended his research to examine thirty-five accidents and found similar results in 80 percent of the accidents (*Journal of the American Society for Psychical Research* 50, no. 3). The odds of this occurring are far too great to be dismissed as chance. Is it possible that the people who missed the train were somehow warned or protected by their guardian angels?

I've learned the hard way to rely on hunches and intuitions. Nowadays, if logic tells me one thing but intuition tells me the opposite, I'll trust my intuition every time.

Meditation

Over the years, many people have told me that the first experience they had of their guardian angel occurred while they were meditating. This is not surprising, as when you meditate, you're in a relaxed, receptive state. This creates the perfect environment for your guardian angel to communicate with you. However, this doesn't happen to everyone who practices meditation. If you're interested in angels, and develop an "angel consciousness," your guardian angel will enjoy connecting with you while you're meditating.

A good way to practice meditation is to sit or lie down comfortably, close your eyes, and breathe normally. Notice how your body moves with each inhalation and exhalation. Whenever you notice your attention is wandering, direct it back to your breathing again. You don't need to force yourself to meditate for hours;

two or three minutes is enough initially, and you can gradually lengthen your meditations as you gain experience.

Prayer

Prayer is an intimate communication with the Divine. The wonderful thing is that anyone can communicate with the Divine this way. You might belong to a particular religion or belong to none. It makes no difference if you're rich or poor, or good or bad. The Divine isn't concerned about what country you live in, what gender you are, what color your skin happens to be, or where you went to school.

You can phrase your prayers in any way you wish. Speak from your heart, and don't worry about grammar. Use a natural tone and words familiar to you. Don't worry about lengthy pauses, either. After all, Jesus said: "Your Father knoweth what things ye have need of, before ye ask him" (Matthew 6:8). Consequently, a silent prayer can be just as effective as a spoken one.

There's a charming Hasidic story about a man who wanted to pray but discovered he had left his prayer book at home. He decided to recite the alphabet five times and let God rearrange the letters into a prayer. God replied: "Of all the prayers I have heard today, this one was the best because it came from a simple and sincere heart" (De Mello, 22).

You can say your prayers wherever you happen to be. You don't need to kneel or visit a church, synagogue, or mosque. You can sit, stand, walk, kneel, or lie down to pray.

One useful way to resolve difficulties in your life is to pray while falling asleep. Tell the Divine what's going on in your life, and include your successes and failures. Ask the Divine to help you resolve problems and achieve goals and ambitions. If you aren't yet communicating regularly with your guardian angel, ask for a closer connection with them. Continue talking to the Divine until you drift off to sleep. Your soul remains awake while you sleep and will receive information and guidance from the Divine.

You can make contact with your guardian angel using prayer. The Bible warns against worshiping angels (Col. 2:18 and Rev. 19:10), but that isn't what this is. All you need do is pray in your normal manner and during the course of the prayer ask the Divine to help you contact your guardian angel.

Once you've made contact with your guardian angel, you might ask your angel to deliver your prayers for you. You can also ask your guardian angel for help, guidance, and to pray with you. Praying with your guardian angel is a comforting and beneficial exercise. Jesus said: "For where two or three are gathered in my name, there am I in the midst of them" (Matthew 18:20). If you're Christian, this means that when you and your guardian angel pray together, Jesus is there with you.

Coincidences, Synchronicity, and Serendipity

I believe that our guardian angels are responsible for many of the coincidences, synchronicities, and examples of serendipity we experience in our lives. It enables them to gain our attention for a specific purpose. They may be offering encouragement, indicating which path you should take, or answering a prayer. The most common signs are small coins, white feathers, ethereal music from an unknown source, beautiful scents, flashing lights, and electronic items turning on and off by themselves. Any strange coincidence could be a sign as well. You need to be alert to notice these. Be particularly aware of anything that occurs a number of times. Finding a small coin might be simply a matter of chance, but if you find a coin every time you go for a walk, it's likely to be a sign. Some years ago, in the middle of winter, I found small white feathers every time I went for a walk. This carried on for some weeks, and I took it for an obvious sign of angelic contact—there were so few birds around, to say nothing of white ones. Whenever you experience anything that could be called a coincidence or an example of serendipity, pause for a few seconds and silently speak to your guardian angel.

You can request signs from your guardian angel. You can either ask for a specific sign, such as a red rose or small piece of amethyst, or you might prefer to leave the sign up to your guardian angel. Ask your angel to choose something that you will immediately recognize as a sign. Fortunately, your angel will continue to send you signs (if necessary) until you finally recognize them.

It's also likely to be a sign if you frequently encounter the same person, apparently by accident, or hear the same song regularly when you turn on the radio.

Angel Numbers

Repeating numbers are often a sign of an angelic presence. It probably doesn't mean anything if you look at your watch just as it reads 11:11. However, if this happens often, it's likely to be a sign from your guardian angel. The numbers might repeat in different ways. You might notice it first on your watch, and then see it again on a license plate, followed by passing a mailbox with the same number. You have to be alert, as angel numbers can appear when you least expect them. You may visit someone and discover their birthday is on the same date as the number you keep seeing. It might be the length of a movie, a model of a car, the time a bus or train is due to arrive or depart, receipts, price tags, or the page you've reached while reading a book. A number that reoccurs apparently at random is called an angel number and is considered a sign that angels are trying to make contact with you.

If you experience this, you can meditate both to find out what the numbers mean and encourage angelic communication. In numerology, numbers possess different vibrational energies, which is why many people use it to interpret the meanings of the numbers. Many people say that repeating numbers such as 333 or 7777 are said to be the most significant angel numbers. They're definitely important, as they contain the concentrated energy of a single digit. However, any combination of numbers can be an angel number.

Your guardian angel number is a three-digit number derived from your month and day of birth. If, for instance, your birthday is on February 16, your guardian angel number would be 216. If your month and day of birth create a two-digit number, such as March 8, you would add those two numbers together and reduce the total to a single digit which would become the third number. In the example of March 8, $3 + 8 = 11$, and $1 + 1 = 2$. In this example, the guardian angel number would be 382. Similarly, if the month and day of birth create a four-digit number, such as November 17, the final two digits are added together and reduced to a single digit. Consequently, people born on November 17 would have a guardian angel number of 118.

Guardian angel numbers can occur randomly, which means that seeing your guardian angel number once or twice probably doesn't mean anything. However, if you see your number three or more times within a short period, it's likely to be a message that your guardian angel wants to communicate with you.

Letters

Writing a letter to your guardian angel is a highly effective way to make contact. Sit down somewhere quiet where you know you won't be disturbed, and write a friendly letter to your guardian angel. Write it as if you're writing to a good friend, which is, of course, exactly what you are doing. You might start, "Dear Guardian Angel," and then write everything you'd like to say. Obviously, it's best to have a purpose in mind as you write, but your letter can be as short or long as you like. If you haven't communicated with your angel before, you might write and ask for a closer connection. If you're already in contact with each other, ask your guardian angel for anything you need. This might include asking for help for people you know. Tell your angel about what's going on in your life. Include information about your family and friends, your hopes and dreams, what's happening at work, and the blessings in your life. Naturally, you should tell your guardian angel about anything that's worrying or bothering you, and ask for help or advice on how to deal with it. You should also tell your angel that you want to develop a closer connection with them. You can tell your guardian angel absolutely anything, as your angel already knows everything about you and won't love you less if you reveal your deepest, darkest secrets. Finish the letter by expressing your love and gratitude to your guardian angel, and sign your name.

The act of writing forces you to clarify everything in your mind. As a result, you might turn some of your words into goals that you can pursue. You might write something simple, such as:

> Dear Guardian Angel,
>
> Thank you for protecting and guiding me. I'm sorry I haven't always paid attention to you, but now I want to get to know you better. Please make contact so that we can become closer. Thank you.
>
> Love from (your name)

I know people who regularly write lengthy letters to their guardian angels, telling them about everything that's going on in their lives. As no one apart from you and your angel will ever see them, you can make your letters as personal as you like.

Once you've written your letter, thank your guardian angel for looking after you. Express your love and sign your name. Seal the letter inside an envelope, and address it "To My Guardian Angel." If you're fortunate, you might make contact with your guardian angel while writing the letter. If that occurs, you can stop writing and start talking about everything that's on your mind. If it doesn't happen, you'll need to "send" the letter to your guardian angel.

Make a small ceremony of sending your letter. Sit down in front of a lit candle with the envelope in your cupped hands. Think about everything your guardian angel does for you, and offer thanks. When you've said everything you wish to say, burn the envelope in the candle flame and watch the smoke carry your message to your guardian angel. Collect the ashes and scatter them outdoors.

Be alert for any signs or other indications that your guardian angel has received your letter. You may notice that your concerns have been resolved, possibly in a way that you didn't expect. Always remember to thank your guardian angel whenever you receive a response of any sort.

Naturally, you need to be careful when doing anything with candles. I like to place my candles on metal trays and always have water available as a precaution in case of an accident.

An alternative method is to seal the letter inside an envelope and then set it aside for at least three days. When you open the envelope and read the letter, you'll read it with different eyes. Some of the issues you raised may have been dealt with by your guardian angel. Something that appeared important when you wrote the letter may no longer seem significant, and you'll be able to dismiss it from your mind. You may also find matters that you need to focus on. These may come from the words you wrote or thoughts that appear in your mind as you read the letter.

Sometimes, I make a ritual of opening and reading the letter a day or two after writing it.

1. Sit down at a table and place a candle on it. Light the candle, and place the envelope in front of it. Place a crystal on top of the letter. (You can use any crystal you wish. There are some suggestions on which crystals to use in the next chapter.)

2. Close your eyes and visualize the light from the candle expanding until it completely surrounds you. Once you sense this, ask your guardian angel to join you. When you sense your angel's presence, open the envelope, remove the letter, and read it aloud. After doing this, replace the letter inside the envelope and place it back on the table. Place the crystal back on top of it.

3. Sit quietly, with your eyes closed, and wait for your guardian angel's response to your letter. You may not receive a specific response but instead notice a feeling that everything will be all right and the situation will be resolved. You might receive a letter in your mind. If this happens, visualize yourself opening the envelope, taking out the letter, and reading it. You might receive a reply clairaudiently. You may not receive a reply immediately. When this occurs, sit quietly for a few minutes. If you haven't received a message by then, realize that the answer will not come immediately, and patience is required.

4. When you feel ready, thank your guardian angel, count slowly from one to five, and open your eyes. Extinguish the candle and carry on with your day.

5. The final step is to carry the crystal around with you. Think of your guardian angel and your request whenever you see or touch it. If you haven't received an answer within three days, write another letter to your guardian angel, and perform the ritual again.

Guardian Angel Box

Many years ago, a good friend of mine made herself a guardian angel box. It's a cardboard box with a lid that originally held a pair of shoes my friend had bought. She decorated the box in bright colors and attached pictures of angels to it on all six sides. Whenever anything upsets or bothers her, she writes a brief note about the problem to her guardian angel and asks for help. She then folds the note into a tiny packet and drops it into the box. The first time she did this, she found she was able to let go of the concern the instant the packet was dropped into the box, something that has continued to occur ever since. When life is going really well for her, the box might be empty for a while. At other times, when there are problems and difficulties in her life, she might have up to a couple of dozen small packets in the box. On a typical week, she'll have four or five packets.

Once a week, usually on a Sunday evening, she holds a small ritual in which she holds the box and talks to her guardian angel, giving thanks for all the hard work her angel does for her. She also thanks her guardian angel for taking care of her concerns. When she's finished her conversation, she goes outside, tips the packets into a metal container, and sets fire to them. She doesn't open any of the packets, as she knows her guardian angel will have taken care of the problems for her.

Angel Journal

An angel journal provides a record of all your communications with your guardian angel. Over time, this will become increasingly valuable, as you'll be able to look back and see how you're progressing. You can write anything you wish in your journal. I like to start by recording the date, time of day, and where I am while I'm writing. Writing in your journal is similar, but not the same as writing a letter to your angel, as you probably won't record news about your home and family life. As soon as possible after talking with your angel, write down everything you can remember about the conversation. Once you've done this, write down your feelings about the meeting and how you felt once the conversation ended.

Automatic Writing

Automatic writing is the process of writing without using your conscious mind. The communication comes through you, rather than by you. You write in the usual way, using pen and paper, but the pen is directed by some power other than your conscious mind. Many books have been written using automatic writing. William Butler Yeats, Sir Arthur Conan Doyle, Alfred Lord Tennyson, Harriet Beecher Stowe, and Gertrude Stein are all examples of well-known authors who experimented with automatic writing.

Anyone can learn to do automatic writing, but it takes practice to become proficient at it. Most people start by drawing random shapes and only gradually start writing words and sentences.

Start by sitting down comfortably with a pen in your writing hand resting comfortably on a sheet of paper. Your wrist should not make contact with the paper, and your writing arm should be bent at a right angle at the elbow. Relax as much as you can and wait to see what happens. You can close your eyes if you wish, but this isn't essential. Ideally, you should feel relaxed, contemplative, and receptive. Many people find they get better results if the room is slightly darkened and they're feeling tired.

After a while, the hand holding the pen will start to move. You must ignore this sensation, as you have started writing unconsciously—the flow will stop as soon as you pay conscious attention to it. The hardest part of automatic writing is letting go of the conscious mind to allow free reign to the unconscious mind. Wait until the pen stops moving before looking at what you've produced.

Don't be concerned about what you produce when you first experiment with automatic writing. Any movement of the pen is good; the more you practice, the better you'll become at it. Once you gain experience, you'll discover that the speed of the writing you produce is amazing, and that you can write for hours on end without feeling tired. Geraldine Cummins (1890–1969), the Irish novelist and spiritual medium, sometimes produced two thousand words an hour by automatic writing (Fodor, 20).

If you find it hard to get started, try holding the pen in your nondominant hand. Some people receive better results when they do automatic writing using the opposite hand to their usual writing hand. You might find it helpful to have a distraction of some sort, such as meditation music or a dull television program. It takes time to become proficient at automatic writing, but it's worth persevering, as the results can be amazing. People have created poems, plays, novels, drawings, paintings, and music using automatic writing.

Once you've gained experience at automatic writing, ask your guardian angel to send you a message using automatic writing. Set your intention for the session. Your intention might be to establish communication with your guardian angel. You might want to ask a question. You might need help of some sort. It doesn't matter what your intention is, as long as you know why you're performing the automatic writing session.

You might also want to surround yourself with protection. You can do this by asking the four great archangels—Raphael, Michael, Gabriel, and Uriel—to surround you with a wall of protection. (This is the Angelic Invocation of Protection, which appears earlier in this chapter.)

Sit down with pen and paper, say a prayer, relax, and wait for the message to come through. You'll be amazed at the information and insights that your guardian angel can give to you using automatic writing. These messages also provide a permanent record of the information that you can refer to whenever necessary.

When the session is over, thank your guardian angel for coming to your aid. If you've surrounded yourself with protection, thank Raphael, Michael, Gabriel, and Uriel too.

Spend a few minutes thinking about the experience you've just had. Follow this by eating a few nuts and raisins, and drinking something, to ensure that you're grounded before carrying on with your day.

Automatic Conversation

Automatic conversation is similar to automatic writing, but usually you remain in control of the writing process. All you need do is write down a question that you'd like your guardian angel to answer. As quickly as possible, write down the first answer that appears in your mind. If you have a number of questions, don't think about the first answer until after you've written down and received answers to all of your questions.

Some people are able to move from conscious writing to automatic writing in a split second. This means they ask the questions consciously, and then their guardian angel takes control of the pen and answers them. While this skill is useful, it's not essential. It's more common for people to ask a question and then write down the first answer that appears in their minds. This answer will be the correct one, as it has been placed into their minds by their guardian angels.

A slight variation of this enables you to receive a detailed answer to a question you have. Write down your question at the top of a sheet of paper. Allow yourself to enter into a quiet, meditative state. Say a prayer, and then speak to your guardian angel. Explain the problem you have, and why you need an answer. Hold the pen in the same way you do for automatic writing and wait for it to move. When the pen stops moving, thank your guardian angel for helping you, and say a short prayer of thanks to the Divine.

Creativity

You can connect with your guardian angel using your natural skills and talents. Whenever you become totally immersed in something you really enjoy, you move into a slightly altered state that makes it easier to connect with the angelic realms. In this state, you can forget about everything else—in my case, even having lunch—instead becoming fully engrossed in what you're doing.

Candle Meditation

This is a wonderful way to contact the angelic kingdom. You can perform it whenever you wish. I enjoy doing it in the evening, with no light other than a candle flame. You can use any candles that appeal to you. I have a selection of different colored candles and sometimes choose a candle because of its color. Usually, though, I instinctively reach for whatever candle feels right for me at the time.

The following is a short list of color associations to help you decide which candle to use.

- Red provides confidence, energy, and passion.
- Orange eliminates fears, doubts, and worries. It also provides motivation.
- Yellow stimulates the mind and helps establish open, honest communication.
- Green relieves stress, impatience, and anger. It also provides stability and contentment.
- Blue helps overcome nervousness and indecision.
- Indigo provides faith and helps you handle family problems.
- Violet provides inner peace and nurtures the soul.
- Pink helps you overcome emotional difficulties and helps you give and receive love.
- Gray helps you overcome mental exhaustion.
- Silver provides confidence and self-esteem.
- Gold eliminates negative feelings about success and financial improvement.

You can use a white candle for any purpose. If you can't decide on a candle color, use a white one.

Place a lit candle on a table about six feet from where you'll be sitting. The flame of the candle should be at about the level of your third eye when you're sitting down. Take a few slow, deep breaths and gaze at the flickering flame. Think of your desire to contact your guardian angel. After a few minutes, you may sense or even catch a glimpse of your angel. When this occurs, start talking to your guardian angel silently or out loud.

Pendulum Dowsing

A pendulum is a small weight attached to a length of chain or thread. This simple device has been used for thousands of years. The ancient Egyptians used it to find the best places to plant their crops, and the ancient Chinese used it to deter evil spirits (Copen, 20–21). The word "dowsing" means to detect something that cannot be found in any other way. Dowsers use a variety of tools, including pendulums, to help them find oil, water, and minerals. I addition to this, they also use them to answer questions, enhance spiritual growth, eliminate negative energy, and to communicate with angels and spirit guides.

Commercially made pendulums are readily available at New Age stores and online. However, you can easily make your own by attaching a small weight to a length of thread or cord. The weight can be made of almost anything—wood, crystal, glass, plastic, and some metals. I often use an old key that I've attached to a chain. My favorite pendulum was made for me by a good friend in Germany; I think of him every time I use it. It consists of a small piece of carved greenstone (New Zealand jade) attached to a loop of cord. I wear it around my neck as an amulet and lucky charm, so I almost always have a pendulum on me whenever I happen to need one.

I also have a number of special pendulums used solely for working with the angelic realms. These are crystal pendulums, as angels respond well to them. My favorite pendulum for communicating with angels is made of selenite attached to a silver chain. Selenite is often used for protection and for helping people to grow spiritually. It is a beautiful translucent white crystal that seems to glow when polished. Celestite, especially pale blue celestite, is frequently used to attract angels, and I have several crystals made with it. Celestite helps people to hear messages from their guardian angels clairaudiently, which means they receive the messages as thoughts inside their heads. Rutilated quartz is known as "angel hair" due to the inclusions of fine rutile, which looks like strands of hair that have been caught inside the crystal. As quartz amplifies angelic communication, this crystal is also popular for enhancing angelic communication.

When you have your pendulum, sit down in front of a table with the chain or cord held between the thumb and index finger of your dominant hand. Rest your elbow on the table, and make sure that no other part of your body is touching it. Your legs should be uncrossed, and your feet should be flat on the floor. The palm of the hand holding the pendulum should face downward, and the pendulum should hang several inches in front of you.

Swing the pendulum gently in different directions. You might start by swinging it in both clockwise and counterclockwise circles, then from side to side, and finally toward and away from you. Doing this helps you become familiar with the pendulum, and the different movements it makes. Experiment by holding the pendulum at different places on the chain or cord to see which feels best for you. You'll probably find that four to five inches is about right. However, you might prefer a shorter or longer length than that. While you're experimenting, try the different movements while holding the pendulum in your other hand.

Once you've become familiar with the different actions that the pendulum can make, stop the movement of the weight with your free hand. When the pendulum is still, ask it which movement indicates a yes or positive response. You can do this silently or out loud. If you're fortunate, your pendulum will immediately move to indicate the positive response. However, this is unlikely if you haven't used a pendulum before. You may find that it moves slightly or doesn't move at all. Be patient and continue asking the pendulum to indicate its positive response. If it hasn't provided a response after five minutes, stop, put the pendulum away, and try again later. It can be frustrating when the pendulum ignores your request. Continue practicing for about five minutes at a time.

If you still have no response after several attempts, temporarily forget about requesting a positive response. Instead, focus on the weight and imagine it moving toward and away from you, or from side to side. Once it starts moving, imagine the swing becoming stronger and watch the movements growing in length. Play with this for a minute or two, and then stop the movement, and ask the pendulum to indicate its positive response. This works most of the time.

If you're still having problems, ask someone who can use a pendulum to place a hand on your right shoulder if you're holding the pendulum in your right hand (or your left shoulder if you're using your left hand). Ask for a positive response, and you'll find the pendulum will move to indicate it. That said, I have never met anyone who can't use a pendulum. All you need do is be patient, suspend disbelief, and allow it to happen. Keep your sense of humor and have fun with these practice sessions. Grim determination makes it almost impossible for the pendulum to move. After your pendulum has responded once, you'll never have problems again.

After receiving your positive response, stop the movements of the weight and ask it to indicate your no or negative response. Follow this by asking it to indicate its responses to "I don't know" and "I don't want to answer." These four responses will probably stay the same for the rest of your life. However, it pays to check them every now and again, especially if you haven't used your pendulum for a while, just in case the movements have changed.

The next step is to ask your pendulum questions that you know the answer to. You might, for instance, ask, "Am I married?" Your pendulum should give a positive response if you are, and a negative response if you aren't. You can ask similar questions about your gender, age, occupation, number of children, and hobbies. You might prefer to ask neutral questions, such as, "Is this month July?"; "Is it raining outside?"; or "Is this carpet blue?"

Once you're getting consistently correct answers from your pendulum, you can start asking questions that you don't know the answers to. A good way to do this is to ask questions about someone who is in the same room as you. This means you can check the pendulum's responses right away. You might ask, "Does (person's name) like broccoli?"; "Does (person's name) speak more than one language?"; or "Does (person's name) like to dance?" Try this test with several people. You'll find that most people will be fascinated with your pendulum and be happy to participate.

You can now ask questions about anything, as long as you're able to check the answers later. If you practice regularly, your accuracy with the pendulum will increase, and in time it will consistently give you the correct information.

When deciding what questions to ask, you need to be careful so that you don't override the movements of the pendulum with your will, which is most likely to occur when you have an emotional investment in the answer. A common example is when a pregnant woman asks if the pendulum can reveal the gender of her unborn baby. If you know that she is hoping for a girl, the pendulum will reflect your feelings and say that it will be a girl, even if that is not the case. If you have any emotional involvement with a question, it's better to ask someone who has no interest in the outcome to use the pendulum for you.

It's important to become used to your pendulum before using it to communicate with your guardian angel. Once you've reached this stage, write down a list of everything you'd like to discuss with your angel. Rearrange this list in order of importance, as you'll probably find that you won't have time to ask all your questions in one session.

1. Set aside about thirty minutes of uninterrupted time. You might like to light a white candle and display a crystal or two to create the right atmosphere for angelic contact.

2. Sit down in a comfortable straight-backed chair facing the candle. Swing your pendulum in a counterclockwise direction and visualize it removing all the negativity in your body, heart, mind, and spirit. When the pendulum stops moving, swing it in a clockwise direction and visualize it attracting positivity into every cell of your body. When it stops moving, close your eyes and either enjoy a few moments of complete silence or say a brief prayer.

3. When you feel ready, speak to your guardian angel. You might say: "Good evening, Guardian Angel. I want to get to know you better, and I also have a few questions I'd like to ask. Are you able to talk to me?"

4. Wait and see what answer you receive. Usually, your pendulum will move in a positive direction, letting you know that your guardian angel is willing to have a conversation with you. It's possible that your pendulum won't move at all, especially if this is the first

time you've tried to contact your guardian angel. Your angel might be testing you to see how sincere you are about establishing a close connection. If this happens, repeat the process on another day and keep doing this until your angel responds. On rare occasions, your pendulum might indicate a negative response. This simply means your guardian angel is busy performing another task or you might be angry, anxious, or stressed about something. When this happens, try again later or on another day when you're feeling at ease and relaxed.

5. Once you've made contact, ask your angel your first question. Phrase it in such a way that it can be answered by one of the four movements the pendulum can make. Thank your guardian angel for responding. Continue asking questions and receiving answers until the time seems right to stop. I find about twenty minutes is ideal.

6. Thank your guardian angel for spending time with you and for answering your questions. Express your love and gratitude, and say how much you're looking forward to your next communication. Smile as you say goodbye.

7. Swing your pendulum in a clockwise direction and send love to the entire world until it stops moving.

8. Sit quietly for a minute or two, snuff out the candle, and carry on with your day.

You're likely to feel excited after this ritual, and hopefully you'll have received answers to some important questions. You can also use this ritual to learn your guardian angel's name. It's a lengthy process, as you need to go through the alphabet one letter at a time, asking your angel if each letter is the first letter of the name. You need to repeat this process as many times as necessary to find out your guardian angel's name. (There are five other ways to learn your guardian angel's name, explained in the next chapter.)

Angel Cards

Whenever you visit a New Age store, you can't help but notice the large variety of angel card decks that are available. Hopefully, you'll see my *Oracle of the Angels* card deck that was published by Llewellyn Publications in 2014. It's not surprising that so many decks are available nowadays, as they are a convenient way to commune with the angelic realms and receive messages from the angels. The cards give the angels the opportunity to provide you with healing and guidance. In the process, you'll also develop your psychic and spiritual awareness.

Although you can easily buy a set of angel cards, you'll find it a rewarding experience to make your own. It puts your own personal energy into the cards. The process itself also strengthens your connection with the angels. You need no artistic skills. You can create a deck of cards using file cards, business cards, note cards, or even small rectangular pieces of paper or cardboard. A visit to a craft store will provide you with many ideas on what to use. I bought some double-blank playing cards for the first deck I made. These are the size of regular playing cards but are blank on both sides. (I've recently checked: these are easy and cheap to buy online.)

On each card, write a word or words on any topic that the angels can help you with (I use colored pencils and markers). You might use cards of different colors and decorate them with stickers of stars, snowflakes, and angels. Recently, I found a set of two dozen rubber stamps of angels in a dollar store and plan to use them next time I make an angel card deck. You might cut pictures out of old magazines and paste them on to the cards. Naturally, if you have artistic skills, you can draw or paint a picture of an angel on every card. Once the cards are finished, you might like to laminate them. I've never done this, but it would make the cards last longer.

I prefer to have blank backs on my cards to ensure that I can't identify any of the cards from the backs after I've shuffled them. However, an acquaintance of mine puts a different colored back onto each of her cards. You might like to do this too. The only disadvantage is that she has to close her eyes when drawing a card.

Your deck can contain as few or as many cards as you wish. You might start off with a small number of cards and gradually add cards as you think of aspects of your life you need help with. The best words are ones you can meditate on or possibly use as part of an affirmation.

As you're creating the deck for your own personal use, you can include anything at all that relates to you and your needs. For instance, if you want to raise your self-esteem, include cards that relate to confidence, resilience, positive self-talk, and self-belief. If you're studying, you might add education, study habits, and concentration. My first deck contained forty cards and gradually grew to about sixty. Here's a list of possible words you might use:

Abundance	Joy
Assertiveness	Light
Balance	Love
Beauty	Meditation
Blessings	Motivation
Communication	Openness

Compassion	Patience
Courage	Peace
Creativity	Play
Energy	Positivity
Enthusiasm	Power
Exercise	Purification
Fairness	Purpose
Faith	Relationship
Forgiveness	Reliability
Freedom	Responsibility
Friendship	Romance
Generosity	Security
Gentleness	Self-discipline
Gratitude	Spontaneity
Growth	Strength
Harmony	Success
Healing	Surrender
Honesty	Tenderness
Hope	Transformation
Humor	Trust
Inner peace	Truth
Insight	Understanding
Inspiration	Vitality
Intuition	Wisdom

The easiest way to use the cards is to mix the cards facedown while asking your guardian angel to help you choose the card that will be most useful for you during the next twenty-four hours. Once you've finished mixing the cards, pull out a card from anywhere in the facedown deck, and place it somewhere where you'll see it several times a day. You might like to carry the card in your purse or wallet. Every time you see it, you will be reminded of your guardian angel and the quality or attribute your angel suggests you should be focusing on today.

At least once during the day, sit down with the card and ask your guardian angel why that particular card was chosen for you. You might like to light a candle or display a few crystals before doing this. I use selenite and celestite, as they both relate well to angels.

Make yourself comfortable. If you're alone, talk out loud to your guardian angel. If there are other people within hearing distance, you might prefer to speak silently. You might like to close your eyes to reduce all possible distractions. Talk in a quiet, conversational way, and pause every now and again to see if your guardian angel responds. You're most likely to receive the answers as thoughts in your mind. You may hear the voice of your angel inside your head. You may hear nothing but experience a sense of knowing that your guardian angel is with you. If you haven't done anything of this sort before, it may seem as though you experienced nothing at all—don't be concerned if this is the case, as it will happen in time as long as you continue this brief meditation on a regular basis. A friend of mine said that she wasn't bothered at all when it took her a few weeks to start a two-way conversation with her guardian angel. "It's like making friends," she told me. "Sometimes it happens instantly, but with other people it can take a while."

Before finishing the session, ask your guardian angel if you should keep the same card for another twenty-four hours, or if you should pull another card.

When you've finished, express your love and thanks to your angel and then carry on with your day. It can be helpful to write down all the insights you learn during these sessions. I also record the date, time, place, how I was feeling, and anything else that seems relevant. Over time, these notes will provide a valuable record of your angelic experiences.

You can also use your angel cards to give readings to yourself and others. Mix the cards until you feel guided to stop. Deal the top three cards from the facedown deck in a row in front of you. The card on the left relates to the past, the center card relates to the present, and the card on the right the future.

Turn over the card on the left and look at it. See what comes into your mind. Trust your intuition, as it is likely to be correct. See how this card relates to matters that have occurred in the past. Turn over the middle card and see what it tells you about the present. Finally, turn over the future card to gain impressions about your future.

Originally, I kept my cards inside the box my blank cards came in. However, as the number of cards increased, I've had to find other ways to protect the cards. At the moment, I keep my cards wrapped in a violet-colored silk handkerchief inside a bag designed to hold tarot cards, found in a New Age store that had a large selection of different colored bags.

IS IT POSSIBLE TO SEE YOUR GUARDIAN ANGEL?

Throughout history, certain people have been able to see angels. It used to be an extremely rare occurrence, but over the last forty years there has been a huge upsurge in the numbers of reports about angel sightings. This may be because angels have become more visible than they used to be. It may be because more people are seeking spirituality. Whatever the reason, a number of possibilities need to be considered when someone claims to have seen an angel.

1. The person actually saw, or experienced, an angel.

2. The person may have been unintentionally misled. This is common in cases where someone received help from a stranger who immediately disappeared after being of service. The stranger may have quietly left, leaving the person who was helped thinking that they had been helped by an angel.

3. The person may have been hallucinating. These are difficult to quantify, as throughout history many famous visions occurred while people were hallucinating. However, if the person is unstable, or under the influence of a mind-affecting substance, the possibility is there that the person is merely constructing the experience in their mind.

4. The person may have a false memory of an angelic experience. This means the person has a memory in their mind that they think is real when it actually isn't. An acquaintance of mine believed she saw an angel at a county fair when she was twelve years old. Over the years, she told many people about her angelic experience. More than thirty years later, a friend who was with her at the county fair told her that it was actually a man wearing white robes who was waiting to go onto the stage. My acquaintance wasn't fabricating the experience. In her mind, she genuinely thought she had seen an angel.

5. The person may have had a spiritual experience of some sort but has exaggerated it to include angels.

6. It's also possible that the person is lying. People lie for all sorts of reasons, and lying about an angelic visitation might be to impress others or make them think that the liar is more spiritually evolved than they actually are.

Because of this, you need to be careful about accepting stories about angels at face value.

Despite this, there are many documented accounts of people who were able to see angels on a regular basis. One of the most famous of these was Padre Pio (mentioned in chapter 1), who started seeing angels as a young child, and by the age of five had decided to devote his life to God. He entered the novitiate of the Capuchin Friars in 1903, and was ordained as a priest in 1910. He received his stigmata, the bleeding wounds that Jesus received on the cross, in the same year. This caused him grave embarrassment, and he prayed for them to go away. As this didn't happen, he started wearing gloves on his hands and stockings on his feet. Padre Pio is one of about three hundred people who have received the stigmata since St. Francis of Assisi received his in 1224.

Padre Pio had a close connection with his guardian angel all the way through his life. He started seeing and conversing with his angel at the age of five. He called his guardian angel *Angelino*, or "little angel," as a term of endearment, rather than the angel's name. In his biography of Padre Pio, Father Alessio Parente wrote: "Padre Pio's spiritual guidance of souls was mostly done through the help and direction of his Guardian Angel" (Parente, 113).

On numerous occasions, Padre Pio's guardian angel protected him when he was attacked by devils. During one of these attacks, his guardian angel took longer than Padre Pio expected to arrive, and he angrily shouted at him. His angel replied that he was always close to him, and that his love would continue even after Padre Pio died. In a letter that he wrote to his spiritual adviser about this, Padre Pio said that his guardian angel was too good, and that he needed to be more grateful to him (Epistolario I. San Giovanni Rotondo, 1987. Letter 102, 311–312).

Padre Pio was able to see other people's guardian angels and encouraged people to send them to him whenever they were experiencing difficulties in their lives. On one occasion, Padre Pio complained to his fellow priests that he'd had no sleep the previous night, as he'd received a constant stream of people's guardian angels, all seeking help for their charges.

On one occasion, a busload of pilgrims who were on their way to visit Padre Pio were forced to stop by a sudden storm in the Apennine Mountains. The pilgrims remembered what Padre Pio had told them and prayed to his angel. When they finally reached San Giovanni Rotondo, where Padre Pio lived, he greeted them by saying, "Well, my children, last night you woke me up and I had to pray for you." His guardian angel had received their prayers and passed them on to Padre Pio (Huber, 68).

The Englishman Cecil Humphrey-Smith was involved in a serious motor accident in Italy. While he was in hospital, one of his relatives went to the telegraph office to send a message to Padre Pio, asking him to pray for Cecil. After filling out the telegram, Cecil's relative paid for it to be sent and was immediately handed a telegram from Padre Pio addressed to Cecil Humphrey-Smith, saying that he was praying for his recovery.

Padre Pio's stigmata disappeared on September 23, 1968, the day he died. Almost 100,000 people attended his funeral. On June 16, 2002, in front of 500,000 people, Pope John II canonized Padre Pio, which means he is now Saint Padre Pio. Throughout his life, Padre Pio made a daily prayer to his guardian angel:

Angel of God,

My guardian,

To whom the goodness

Of the Heavenly Father entrusts me,

Enlighten, protect and guide me

Now and forever,

Amen.

Another example is Lorna Byrne, the Irish spiritual teacher, author, and philanthropist, who has seen angels since she was a small child. She originally saw guardian angels as youthful humanlike figures who stood about three paces behind their charges and sometimes completely surrounded them with unconditional love. They paid little attention to other people's guardian angels, instead focusing entirely on the person they were looking after. Lorna has never seen anyone who doesn't have a guardian angel. As she grew older, she gradually stopped seeing people's guardian angels in human form; now she sees them as pillar-like beams of light that open up to reveal the guardian angel inside whenever it has something to say. Lorna has recounted her experiences with angels in a series of best-selling books that have made her famous around the world (see bibliography for a selection of titles).

Padre Pio and Lorna Byrne are two examples of what is possible. It's exceptionally rare for anyone to see one angel, let alone to see many on a regular basis. Most of the people I've spoken to who have seen angels did so in the form of dreams, visions, and creative visualizations. All of them saw their guardian angels, some were able to see a large choir of angels, and a few reported seeing Archangel Michael or Archangel Raphael.

You may be able to see your guardian angel in your dreams if you say to yourself before dropping off to sleep: "Tonight I'm going to see my guardian angel in my dreams, and when I wake up, I'll remember everything that happened." If you do this regularly, you may be fortunate enough to see your guardian angel.

A friend of mine did this for several weeks without success, and then saw her guardian angel unexpectedly while walking across a park on her way to her local shops. She attributed the delay to the feeling of expectancy she'd built up while asking her guardian angel to appear in her dreams.

Many people see their guardian angels while performing a creative visualization. The major criticism of this technique is that you may create a picture of your guardian angel in your mind rather than see your actual guardian angel. This criticism is valid, but you can confirm that you're speaking with your guardian angel by asking at least one question and listening carefully to the answer.

Think of the questions you intend to ask before doing the visualization. Make them as clear and specific as possible. Tell your guardian angel some of your hopes and dreams, and ask for angelic guidance on what you should do with them.

Try not to have any preconceived ideas about what your guardian angel will look like. You know that angels can appear in any shape or form they choose, and your angel might surprise you by appearing in a form you didn't expect.

Set aside about thirty minutes of time when you know you won't be disturbed. Wear loose-fitting clothes, and make sure the room is pleasantly warm.

1. Sit down in a comfortable chair, close your eyes, and take several slow, deep breaths, holding each inhalation for a few moments before exhaling slowly. Allow yourself to let go of all the tensions and stresses of the

day, and let yourself relax more and more with each exhalation.

2. When you feel completely relaxed, picture a beautiful place in your mind. It could be somewhere you've visited in the past or a scene created in your mind—it doesn't matter how it appears, as long as you feel peaceful, safe, and happy in this pleasant place. Make the scene as detailed as possible by adding sounds, smells, and movement, such as fluffy clouds and a gentle breeze. If you wish, you can also include people.

3. Smile as you walk inside the scene you created. Notice how happy, contented, and excited you feel, as you sense you're about to meet your guardian angel.

4. Pause for a few moments and then turn around in a complete circle, noticing how beautiful the scene is from every angle. As you do this, a flash of movement catches your eye. You turn back and see your guardian angel.

5. You're overcome for a moment, but quickly regain your composure, and say, "Thank you for making yourself visible to me," to your guardian angel. Once you've finished the greetings, it's time to ask your questions. You may not receive a reply the first time you do this. If you do, you may hear your angel answering your question. You might receive the answer as a thought in your head, as a flash of intuition, or even as a sudden sense of knowing. The most important part of this visualization is to make contact and see your guardian angel. Consequently, it doesn't matter if you don't

receive an answer to all or any of your questions. You'll have plenty of time to ask them again in the future.

6. Offer your thanks again, and mention how thrilled you are to have made contact and seen your guardian angel. Say how much you're looking forward to seeing your guardian angel in the future, and finish with a sincere goodbye.

7. Turn around in a full circle again. Notice that your guardian angel is no longer visible, and the beautiful scene is slowly fading away. Remain sitting comfortably for a few minutes to think about the experience you've just had.

8. When you feel ready, silently count from one to five and open your eyes.

Contacting your guardian angel for the first time is the hardest part of the process. Once you've established communication and are communicating with your special angel, you'll be able to start working with them. We'll look at that in the next chapter.

WORK WITH YOUR GUARDIAN ANGEL

In this chapter, you'll learn how to find out your guardian
angel's name, how your guardian angel can heal you physically, emotionally, and spiritually, aid spiritual growth, release
emotional baggage, dissolve limiting beliefs, gain self-esteem, and
even how to mend a broken heart.

HOW TO LEARN YOUR
GUARDIAN ANGEL'S NAME

In the early years of Christianity, scholars assumed that angels
worked in the same way that any large organization does, with
the head person at the top of a pyramid, and the least important
people at the bottom. They called this organizational structure
the hierarchy of angels. No one knows if this is how the realm of
angels works, but it seems that the individual angels pay it much
mind, as they're eternally focused on the tasks they have to do.
They don't have much interest in whichever specific group they
have been placed. For the same reason, angels are not particularly
interested in names, a purely human construct. Your guardian
angel is concerned solely with *you* and your progress in this incarnation. Consequently, your angel will respond to you no matter

what name you use for them. In fact, the response will be just as fast if you simply call on "Guardian angel" or "My angel."

One of the most commonly asked questions I receive once people hear about my interest in angels is, "Can you tell me my guardian angel's name?" Due to our natural human desire to know the names of people with whom we interact, it isn't surprising that I am asked this so frequently—after all, our guardian angel is our closest friend. It's natural to want to know their name or what they may be called.

Fortunately, your guardian angel is happy to give you this information. All you need to do is ask. The name may come to you in a dream or as a thought in your mind. You can ask for your guardian angel's name while automatic writing or dowsing with a pendulum. If the name doesn't come to you using any of these methods, there are other ways to learn it. If you've already established a close connection with your guardian angel, you can ask for the name before or after discussing other matters. If you haven't reached that stage yet, here are five time-tested methods that will help you. Read them all first, and then decide which method appeals to you most.

GUARDIAN ANGEL MEDITATION

You can perform this meditation whenever you wish, but evening is usually a good time because it is quiet, allowing you to enjoy about thirty minutes of undisturbed time to relax and communicate with your guardian angel. Doing this in the evening has another advantage as well. Several times during the day, you can say to yourself, "Tonight I'm going to learn my guardian angel's name." This builds up a positive expectancy inside yourself that you'll be enjoying a conversation with your guardian angel and will learn their name.

The place where you meditate should be comfortable and warm. Wear loose-fitting clothes and make sure wherever you will sit has a straight-backed chair. You can decorate your surroundings if you wish. You might, for instance, like to light a candle or surround yourself with a circle of gemstones or crystals. You might use an essential-oil burner to scent the room.

1. Start by performing the Angelic Invocation of Protection in chapter 3.

2. Sit down comfortably in the chair with both feet flat on the floor, hands resting in your lap. Close your eyes and take three slow, deep breaths.

3. Visualize yourself with a strong connection to the Divine through a pure white light that reaches down from the heavens and enters your body at the top of your head. Once you can sense this and feel a divine, healing light filling you with pure live-giving energy, visualize roots coming out from the soles of your feet that burrow deep into the earth, making you feel safe, secure, and grounded.

4. Focus on your breathing again and take another three slow, deep breaths. Each time you breathe in, visualize that you're filling every cell of your being with loving energy from the angels. With each exhalation, feel yourself relaxing as you let go of all tension, stress, and negativity.

5. Mentally scan your body and consciously relax any areas of tension. You can do this by focusing on the tense area until the muscles dissolve and let go. Alternatively,

you might prefer to tighten the muscles in the area that needs to relax and purposefully release the tension as you exhale.

6. When you feel totally relaxed, focus on the area around your heart (your heart chakra), and express your gratitude to the Divine for all the blessings you have in your life, as well as the gift of life itself. Open your heart and allow the angelic realms to fill your soul with peace and divine love.

7. In this calm, peaceful, relaxed state, imagine yourself standing at the top of a beautiful staircase. There are ten steps leading down to the place where you'll talk with your guardian angel. It's the most beautiful setting you can possibly imagine. Take hold of the handrail, and as you count each step from ten down to one, allow yourself to double your relaxation with each step. Ten, nine, eight, seven, six, five, four, three, two, and one.

8. As you leave the bottom step, sense the presence of your guardian angel. Imagine your guardian angel is standing beside you and that you can feel yourself surrounded by compassion, tenderness, and love. You might sense your angel's warmth, see beautiful colors, detect a beautiful scent, or hear celestial music.

9. Visualize your guardian angel leading you to a place where you can sit together and have a heart-to-heart talk. Even if this is the first time you've communicated with your guardian angel, you'll feel as if you've been good friends forever—in fact, you have been.

10. Enjoy the conversation, and when you feel the time is right, ask your angel, "What is your name?" You're likely to feel a strong emotion in your throat or heart as you wait for the reply. This is because you've opened your throat and heart chakras. Your throat chakra controls communication and self-expression, while your heart chakra looks after empathy, compassion, and love.

11. If the time is right, your guardian angel will respond and answer your question. There's no need to be concerned if you don't receive a reply; all you need do is ask the question again at a later time.

12. Continue your conversation with your guardian angel for as long as you wish. Express your love, and give thanks for everything your angel has done for you over the years, especially the constant guidance and protection.

13. When you sense that it's time to say goodbye, thank your angel again and say how much you're looking forward to your next conversation.

14. Look around at the beautiful setting around you, take a slow, deep breath, and then count from one to five. Open your eyes when you feel ready, and take a minute or two to think about the experience you've had.

15. Stand up and thank Raphael, Michael, Gabriel, and Uriel for protecting you while you performed the meditation. Say goodbye to them and carry on with your day.

It's a good idea to write down everything you can remember about your conversation with your guardian angel right away lest you forget it.

Many people feel a little bit spacey after performing this meditation. Eat and drink something to ground yourself again before continuing with your day. I usually eat a handful of raisins and nuts and drink a glass of water while thinking about what I gained from the meditation.

You're likely to feel emotional afterward, which is perfectly natural. You're also likely to feel full of love and compassion for yourself, and others. Consequently, you might like to communicate with a few loved ones after the meditation. You don't need to tell them what you've been doing (unless you want to), but do be sure to tell these people what they mean to you and how much you appreciate them. A few weeks ago, a good friend closed an email to me by writing: "I am so glad to have you in my life." I was incredibly moved by his words. Most of the time, we forget to express our kind and loving thoughts to others. You'll find this much easier to do if you communicate with the special people in your life shortly after performing this meditation.

ANGELIC BIBLIOMANCY

The term "bibliomancy" refers to divination using a book, usually a bible or some other holy book. The person seeking a message opens the book to a random page and either closes their eyes or turns away before touching somewhere on the page. The sentence or paragraph that the finger indicates is interpreted to answer the question or provide insights into the future.

Angelic bibliomancy uses a similar method to learn the name of your guardian angel. It uses your angel's help, plus a combination of bibliomancy and your intuition. The first step is to choose a suitable book. If you're religious, you might use the Bible, the Torah, the Koran, or some other spiritual book. You can use any spiritual book as long as it relates to your own beliefs. Alternatively, you might prefer to use a dictionary or a book of quotations. I sometimes use a book containing the thoughts and advice of Marcus Aurelius (121–180), the Roman emperor and philosopher. Another possibility is to choose a book that you love or is important to you for any reason.

1. Start by performing the Angelic Invocation of Protection in chapter 3.

2. Sit down comfortably with the book you're going to use; I always face east while doing rituals of this sort. Have a pen and paper close at hand. Close your eyes and take several slow deep breaths to help you relax and quieten your mind. Think about your desire to learn your guardian angel's name, and ask your angel to help you receive it during the ritual.

3. When you feel ready, open the book at a random page. Make sure that it actually is random—a favorite book is likely to open at a page you frequently refer to. One alternative is to riffle through the pages and stop when you feel like it. You might like to insert a bookmark or piece of card between two pages. If your book can lay open flat, you'll have a choice of two pages. If not, decide which page you're going to use and hold the book partially open with your non-dominant hand.

4. Once you've chosen the page, close your eyes or turn away, and place the tip of your index finger onto the

page. Open your eyes and see what word on the page you randomly selected. Write down the first letter of this word. This is likely to be the first letter of your guardian angel's name.

5. Repeat steps three and four until your intuition tells you to stop. This is most likely to happen after you've written down three to six letters.

6. As there are twenty-one consonants and only five vowels, chances are that most—and possibly all—the letters you've written down are consonants. Using your intuition again, place vowels between some or all of the consonants to create a series of letters that you can pronounce. If, for instance, the bibliomancy produced the letters T, S, L, and K, you might add vowels to form TASELUK or TISALK. If the letters are RKOFT, you might add just one vowel to create, for instance, RIKOFT or REKOFT. You might add two vowels to create RAKOFET or RUKOFIT. With some combinations of letters, you may not need to add any additional vowels to create a word you can pronounce: for example, ABSOR, KATO, and TOBRAN.

7. The final step is to add the letters EL or ON at the end of the sequence of letters you've created. You may have noticed that most angelic names end with these letters. Using the examples we've created, TASELUK would become TASELUKEL or TASELUKON, and RIKOFT would become RIKOFTEL or RIKOFTON.

8. Ask your guardian angel if you have worked out their correct name. If necessary, repeat step 6 until you've successfully worked it out. After you've discovered

your guardian angel's name, thank your angel for revealing it to you and say a short prayer of thanks to the Divine for enabling you to learn it.

9. Thank your guardian angel by name for all the help you've received. Thank the archangels Raphael, Michael, Gabriel, and Uriel for their help and say good-bye to them. Pause for a minute or two before getting up and carrying on with your day.

YOUR ANGEL CRYSTAL

This method involves using a crystal or gemstone that you can dedicate to your guardian angel. The stone should be attractive and feel pleasant to hold and fondle. You should ideally be able to hold it in your closed hand. You may already own a suitable crystal that you could use. Or you may prefer to look for a crystal that you'll use solely when working with your guardian angel. If you do, look for a crystal that feels comfortable when you hold it. You'll probably have some idea as to the color, size, and type of crystal that works best for you. However, keep an open mind and trust your intuition. I often return home with a crystal that's completely different to the one I had in mind. That's because the crystal I bought "spoke" to me when I looked at it, touched it, or held it.

Angels respond positively to all crystals, but some are said to be better than others. Here are a few crystals that have strong angelic associations:

Celestite

Celestite comes in a variety of colors, ranging from white to brown. The best color for working with your guardian angel is pale blue. Celestite helps you to communicate with your guardian angel clairaudiently.

Selenite

Selenite is a translucent white crystal that glows with a special radiance when polished. Many people use selenite for protection and for communicating with Archangel Gabriel. It's also a good crystal to establish communication with your guardian angel.

Rutilated Quartz

Rutilated quartz is often called "angel hair," as the inclusions of fine rutile look like strands of hair that have become trapped inside the crystal. Quartz amplifies any communications you have with the angels, making it easier to send and receive messages.

Mangano Calcite

Mangano calcite is a beautiful pink-and-white crystal that enhances inner peace, compassion, and love. Because of its association with love, many people hold it over their heart chakras while working with it. It encourages warm and loving communication with your guardian angel.

Angelite

Angelite is a lilac blue-colored stone often found with pure white flecks. It was first discovered in Peru in 1987. It is formed from celestite that has been compressed for millions of years. Many people place it under their pillows when they want to receive angelic messages in their sleep. However, you can also use it to encourage communication with your guardian angel at any time. Angelite is a soft stone and should be kept away from water.

Green Prehnite

Prehnite is usually pale green in color but can also be white, gray, brown, and almost colorless. Green prehnite enhances precognition, helps people involved in healing, and encourages angelic communication.

The above are suggestions only; you can use any crystal you wish. The best crystal is one that "feels" right, one that relates to you and makes you feel positive and happy.

If you have a good selection of crystals to choose from, take a few slow, deep breaths and then pick up each crystal that appeals to you with your non-dominant hand, one at a time. You might experience a sense of warmth or coolness when holding a particular crystal, or it might seem to gently pulse in your hand. You might experience a tingling sensation in your hand when you hold it. Or you may experience none of these sensations but have a sense of knowing that a particular crystal is the right one for you. If you use a pendulum, you could hold it over each of the crystals in turn to determine which one is the right one for you.

Before using your crystal, you need to cleanse it to eliminate any negative energies that it may have picked up from anyone who handled it before you bought it. There are a number of ways to do this:

1. Light a candle and pass your crystal as quickly as you can through the flame. This is a good method if you were born under a fire sign (Aries, Leo, Sagittarius).

2. Bury your crystal in earth for at least twenty-four hours. Wash it in pure spring water (bottled is fine) and pat it dry afterward. This is a good method if you belong to an earth sign (Taurus, Virgo, Capricorn).

3. Light sage incense and hold your crystal in the smoke for about thirty seconds. This is a good method for people who belong to an air sign (Gemini, Libra, Aquarius).

4. Hold your crystal under a source of running water for about a minute. Rain water works well. Bottled spring water is also good if you don't live close to a spring or stream. You can also use water from a faucet. However, check to make sure that you can do this with your crystal. Angelite, celestite, prehnite, and selenite should not be cleansed with water. This is a good method for people belonging to a water sign (Cancer, Scorpio, Pisces).

5. Natural light is a good way to cleanse tumbled stones. Place your stone directly on the earth where it will be exposed to light from the moon and the sun. Make sure it's somewhere safe where it won't be disturbed by people or wildlife. Place it in position at dusk, and pick it up again between 10:00 and 11:00 a.m. the next day. Wash the stone in fresh water and pat it dry. Remember to check the weather forecast before doing this, as good weather is required.

6. You can also cleanse your crystal with your breath. Hold the stone in the palm of your dominant hand and inhale deeply through your nose. Hold the stone close to your nose and exhale several short, forceful breaths from your nose onto the stone. You may have to repeat this a number of times, exposing different parts of the crystal to your breath each time. It takes about thirty seconds to cleanse a crystal using this method.

Once your stone has been cleansed, you can dedicate it to your guardian angel. The simplest way to do this is to stand outdoors with the crystal in your nondominant hand. While looking at the crystal, say something along the lines of: "I dedicate this crystal to my guardian angel to enhance our connection and increase my receptivity to all messages my special angel sends to me. I ask that this crystal always be surrounded by love and light. Thank you."

Carry the crystal with you for at least seven days to increase your connection with your guardian angel. After that, keep it in a pocket or purse where you'll see it or feel it several times a day. Whenever you need to contact your guardian angel, touch, rub, or hold the crystal to establish an immediate connection.

You might prefer to dedicate your crystal by performing a brief ritual. Place the crystal in the center of your altar. (If you don't have an altar, a small table works just as well.) Situate your altar so that you face east while working at it. Place three white candles around the crystal, one on either side and the other behind it. As always, be careful when using candles, and have a container of water nearby, just in case an accident occurs.

1. Perform the Angelic Invocation of Protection in chapter 3.

2. Light the candles while thinking of your intention to dedicate the crystal to your guardian angel.

3. Gently hold the crystal while saying: "I dedicate this crystal to my guardian angel to enhance our connection, and increase my receptivity to all messages from my guardian angel. I dedicate this crystal to the ultimate good and ask that this crystal always be surrounded by love and light. Thank you."

4. Pick up the crystal in your nondominant hand. Smile at it, and show the crystal to the archangels of the four directions: Raphael in the east, Michael in the south, Gabriel in the west, and Uriel in the north.

5. Place the crystal on the altar again and gently stroke it as you talk to your guardian angel. You might say, "This crystal is for both of us, to help us communicate clearly with each other. My intention is that this will bring us even closer together. I love you, my dear guardian angel. Thank you for being with me every moment of this life. I am more grateful than words can say." Speak for as long as you wish.

6. Pick up the crystal and hold it as high as you can in your cupped hands. Say: "I ask for divine love and protection for me, my guardian angel, and this crystal, which will be working with us and for us. Thank you."

7. Place the crystal on the altar again. Say a short prayer and stand in silence for a minute or two. When you feel ready, extinguish the candles, thank the four great archangels for their protection, and finish the ritual.

The final stage is to use the crystal to send messages to your guardian angel and receive replies and messages. You'll have to carry the crystal with you for at least a week after dedicating it before using it to communicate with your guardian angel.

In time, you'll find that you can establish an instant connection with your angel simply by touching or stroking your crystal. Initially, you'll need to spend a few minutes holding your crystal while thinking of your guardian angel and the question or questions you want to ask. Your crystal will let you know the instant that communication has been made. You'll sense a subtle change such as a change in temperature, a tingling sensation, or simply a sense of knowing, when it happens.

Once the connection has been made, talk to your guardian angel while holding or touching your crystal. You can do this out loud if you're on your own, or in your mind. Your guardian angel will be happy to hear from you; speaking silently or out loud makes no difference.

During this first communication, ask your angel to give you a sign during the next few days. Be alert for anything out of the ordinary. You might see more of the usual signs of angelic presence such as butterflies, feathers, beautiful smells, and small coins, but you could also feel changes in your crystal or see interesting coincidences that relate purely to you.

It's now time to ask for your guardian angel's name. In your next session, ask: "Dear Guardian Angel, I'd love to know your name. Please let me know what it is." Again, be alert for any signs from your angel. You may notice the same name appearing numerous times. You might see or hear an unusual name that catches your attention. A billboard that you've hardly noticed before may suddenly catch your eye and you read a name or word that intrigues you. You might read something and pause at a particular word for no apparent reason.

Hopefully you'll receive a name this way and know beyond a shadow of doubt that it is the name of your guardian angel. However, it's also possible to receive a name this way yet have doubts that it is your angel's name. If that's the case, you'll want confirmation that it is actually the name of your guardian angel. You can do this by asking for a sign that the name is correct. This may sound like a tedious and slow way to learn your guardian angel's name, but remember that you'll be developing a closer connection with your guardian angel every time you use your crystal. Over time, you'll find that you'll be able to hear messages clairaudiently. When that happens, you won't need to ask for signs; you'll receive an immediate reply in your thoughts or as a small voice, either inside your head or beside your ear.

Colorful Invocation

This is an enjoyable way to contact your guardian angel. If you're fortunate, you might see your special angel in your mind's eye while you're performing it.

1. Start by creating a "magic circle," and place a chair in the center.

2. Perform the Angelic Invocation of Protection in chapter 3.

3. Sit down on a straight-backed chair, facing east, in the center of your magic circle. Rest your hands in your lap, and place your feet flat on the ground (or floor).

4. Close your eyes and take three slow, deep breaths. Each time you breathe in, think "relaxation in." When you exhale, think "tension and stress going out." Continue taking slow, deep breaths. Consciously relax all the muscles in your body, starting with your toes and finishing at the top of your head. Once you've done this, mentally scan your body to make sure that you are completely relaxed. Allow any areas that are still tense to relax as you focus on them.

5. When you feel totally relaxed, pay attention to your breathing again. Imagine that you're breathing in divine energy each time you inhale. As you exhale, imagine that each exhalation is creating an invisible bubble of

air around you that grows larger and larger with each exhalation. When you feel that you are totally surrounded by this imaginary bubble of air, mentally fill it with your favorite color to make the bubble visible.

6. Enjoy the sensations in your body that this color provides. Mentally change the color, and enjoy the feelings that this different color brings to you. Experiment with different colors and enjoy the different sensations that they provide.

7. Once you've experimented with all the colors that appeal to you, visualize the bubble returning to your favorite color. Take a deep breath, hold it for a few seconds, and exhale slowly. As you exhale, invite your guardian angel to join you. Visualize your angel as clearly as you can inside the bubble. You might see them in your mind's eye. Alternatively, you might experience a sense of knowing that your guardian angel is with you.

8. Allow yourself to become familiar with the scene. Feel the loving energy of your guardian angel and enjoy the feelings it creates in every cell of your body. When you feel ready, start talking to your guardian angel. Thank your angel for helping and guiding you as you've progressed through life. If you have a specific need, discuss it with your angel, whatever it may be. You can ask your guardian angel anything at all. Your guardian angel will listen carefully to what you say and respond with useful insights that will help you resolve your concerns. You can talk with your guardian angel for as long

as you wish. Remember to ask your guardian angel to tell you their name.

9. After you've covered everything you wanted to discuss, thank your guardian angel once again for their help and support, and say goodbye. Watch the bubble slowly dissipate until it disappears. Take three slow, deep breaths, and open your eyes.

10. Remain seated for a minute or two until you feel ready to return to your everyday life. Stand up when you feel ready. Thank the four great archangels for protecting you while you were performing the ritual, and dismiss them one at a time, starting with Archangel Raphael, followed by Michael, Gabriel, and Uriel.

Don't hurry back to your daily tasks. Eat and drink something to ground yourself first, and then relax for a few minutes before continuing with your day.

WALKING WITH YOUR GUARDIAN ANGEL

This is my favorite way to communicate with my guardian angel. You can use it to learn your guardian angel's name, but more importantly, it enables you to enjoy a conversation with your guardian angel whenever you wish.

Allow at least thirty minutes for the walk. You can walk anywhere at all, but if possible, choose somewhere quiet and peaceful where you're unlikely to encounter anyone you know. Walk for a minute or two while thinking about your guardian angel and the matters you'd like to discuss together. Be positively expectant that your angel will soon join you. Chances are, you'll sense that your guardian angel is walking beside you and may have started talking to you. If not, you can say something to get the conversation going. If you haven't felt your angel's presence after a few minutes, fondle your crystal, ask your guardian angel to join you, and immediately start talking. Soon your guardian angel will respond. At any time during one of these conversations, casually ask your guardian angel for their name.

Instead of starting a conversation, you can open your mind and be alert for any messages that come into your mind. You can talk silently or speak out loud when walking with your angel. I do both depending on where I'm walking. Nowadays, many people talk on their phones while walking, which means no one is likely to notice if you walk down a suburban street while talking out loud. I live on the edge of a city and do most of my walking out in the country where I seldom encounter anyone else. I talk out loud when doing this, but it's become a habit for me to talk silently while walking along suburban streets.

You can discuss anything at all while walking with your guardian angel. Naturally, you should express your love and gratitude for everything your angel does for you. You'll find that you'll be able to enjoy both light-hearted, casual conversations as well as deep, philosophical discussions. Your guardian angel has endless patience and will be happy to explain things to you over and over again, whenever necessary.

You don't need to be walking to enjoy a conversation with your guardian angel. You can touch your crystal and communicate with your angel anywhere, at any time. I've talked with my guardian angel on buses, trains, airplanes, and a variety of other places. You'll find your guardian angel will be delighted to talk with you at almost any time.

HEALING WITH YOUR GUARDIAN ANGEL

Your guardian angel wants you to lead the very best life you possibly can. To do that, you need to feel well spiritually, emotionally, mentally, and physically.

You can ask your guardian angel to help you heal pain, no matter what the cause might be. For instance, if you are suffering from eczema, a painful and itchy skin condition, you can ask your angel to give you relief. You may likely feel relief for a while, but it will ultimately return. This is because the underlying reason behind the condition needs to be discovered and addressed before you can be totally healed. Your guardian angel will be happy to help you with this and will lead you to places and situations relating to your health concern. You may, apparently by chance, meet a naturopath who recommends certain medications that will help. You might find yourself buying certain food items that you wouldn't normally purchase. You could have a desire to eat raw vegetables, or dramatically increase your intake of water. Whenever something like this occurs, ask your guardian angel if they led you to whatever it happens to be. If the answer is yes, ask any further questions you might have to find out how these changes will affect and ultimately heal your condition.

Many health problems begin with negative emotions. Cancer, diabetes, and heart problems can be caused by negative thoughts and feelings. Stubbornness and rigidity can cause neck problems. Fear of change and new ideas sometimes cause stomach problems. Many years ago, I learned that lower back pain can be caused by financial problems. A few hours after my bank manager turned down my request for an increased overdraft, I experienced a sudden pain in my lower back. It continued intermittently until my financial situation improved. Your guardian angel can help you handle difficult emotions to allow healing to take place.

Obviously, you should consult a medical practitioner for all health problems. In addition, you can ask your guardian angel to help you regain your health and energy. Follow your doctor's advice and be alert to any messages you receive from your guardian angel. You can help the process by being kind to yourself, keeping as positive as you can, and expressing gratitude everywhere you go.

Here's a ritual that you can use to aid self-healing. Note that this can be a very emotional ritual, perhaps more so than the others you have done up to this point.

1. Start by performing the Angelic Invocation of Protection in chapter 3.

2. Sit in a straight-backed chair inside your magic circle, face east, and ask your guardian angel to join you. When you sense that your angel is by your side or in front of you, ask for help. (This may sound obvious, but your guardian angel won't intervene unless you ask. I've been guilty of this a number of times over the years. There's no point in being stoic and putting up with pain when you don't need to!) Ask your angel for help, comfort, and healing.

3. You may experience a sensation in your heart when you ask for help, comfort, and healing. This is caused by your heart chakra. You can open your heart chakra by reciting positive affirmations, such as, "I am open to love," "I love myself," "I forgive myself and others," and "I love everyone unconditionally." Repeating these affirmations serves two purposes: it opens your heart chakra and it also allows your guardian angel's love and healing vibrations to heal your pain. While your heart

chakra is open, you can express your gratitude and love to your special angel.

4. Be open to receive the healing. You must want to be healed. Some people enjoy being unwell in order to gain attention and sympathy they might not otherwise receive. Consequently, they have no great desire to be healthy and well again. Your guardian angel wants you to be fit and healthy, too, and constantly surrounds you with love and healing energy. Allow a few minutes for this energy and love to permeate into every cell of your body.

5. Now see that directly in front of you is the great Archangel Raphael, he of healing. Ask him to fill you with his healing energy. Enjoy the sensation of being completely surrounded by his love and energy for as long as you wish. Thank him sincerely for his help and love.

6. Thank your guardian angel sincerely for all the love, help, and support you've received throughout your life. Thank your angel for helping you to heal your body, mind, and spirit. Ask your angel if there's anything else you need to know to help the healing process. Ask any other questions you may have. When you've finished the conversation, thank your guardian angel once more, and say goodbye. This means that you're ending the ritual and you no longer need your guardian angel inside the magic circle. You know that your angel will be close by, watching over you as always.

7. Thank the four great archangels for protecting you while you've been conducting the ritual. Say a special thank-you to Archangel Raphael as you close the ritual.

Relax for a minute or two, and make sure you're feeling confident and positive before getting up. Eat and drink something as soon as possible after performing the ritual. Repeat this ritual as often as possible until you're feeling healthy and well again.

Your guardian angel will also help you heal others. However, you need to be careful when doing this, as the illness might be something that the person needs to experience in this incarnation.

ADVICE FROM YOUR GUARDIAN ANGEL

Your guardian angel wants you to lead a fulfilled and happy life. To do this, you need to be healthy in body and mind. If you're suffering from physical pain, it means you're experiencing unpleasant sensations in your body. Although pain is never welcome, it's a sign that you need to pay more attention to your body and find a way to resolve the situation and alleviate the pain. Fortunately, most pain can be treated and controlled or cured. Sadly, some forms of pain are chronic and cannot be cured.

Emotional pain can be just as painful as physical pain. Grief, heartache, anxiety, loneliness, anger, rejection, infidelity, and betrayal are all good examples. Many people try to handle these problems with alcohol and drugs or pretend that the problem doesn't exist. These solutions never work and frequently lead to depression and physical illness.

No matter what form it takes, pain never occurs without a reason. Painkillers can temporarily mask the problem but do not heal it. Consequently, you must seek the best professional help you can to alleviate the pain and hopefully resolve the problem. In addition, you should ask your guardian angel for help and advice. Your angel will guide you to the people who are best equipped to heal you. Your angel will also help you find the source of the pain and tell you what you can do to relieve it in a way that serves your greatest good. If you ask, your angel will let you know why you're experiencing pain in your life.

Your guardian angel's advice might be as simple as telling you to let go of something you've been desperately hanging on to. Hanging on to something that no longer serves you inevitably causes suffering and pain. Once you let go, you'll be able to start moving forward once more. You can work on forgiving yourself and others and start loving yourself again.

Your angel will let you know if there is a higher purpose behind your pain. There is a divine plan for you; strange as it may sound, pain and illness might provide the necessary impetus to force you to rethink your path in life and discover what you're meant to achieve in this incarnation.

Here's a ritual you can perform whenever you need to reduce pain or regain your health.

1. Start by performing the Angelic Invocation of Protection in chapter 3.

2. Sit down comfortably in a straight-backed chair facing east, with both feet flat on the floor and your hands resting on your lap. Close your eyes and take three slow, deep breaths.

3. Ask your guardian angel to help you perform a healing ritual. Continue taking slow, deep breaths until your guardian angel responds. You may feel a light touch, a sense that you're surrounded by your angel, or simply a sense of knowing that your guardian angel is with you and more than willing to help you.

4. As you inhale, imagine a stream of pure white light descending and entering into your body through your

crown chakra. Your crown chakra is a powerful energy center inside your aura at the top of your head. As you exhale, feel this pure white light entering your body, revitalizing and healing every cell of every organ it touches. You sense the healing in your head first, but with each inhalation it spreads into your arms and shoulders, then into your chest and back. It spreads down into your abdomen, down each leg to the tips of your toes. Each inhalation provides more light energy, and with each exhalation, light gradually spreads to more and more parts of your body until you are full of pure white light.

5. The white light continues to descend onto your crown chakra even after your body is full of white light energy. It now spreads all over you and gradually creates a large ball of pure white light that completely surrounds you. You feel pleasantly warm, safe, and secure inside the ball of light.

6. Mentally scan your body to make sure that the light has spread to every part of your being. Visualize the white light spreading into any area that needs it.

7. Ask your guardian angel to help the white light provide even more healing energy to any areas of pain or disease.

8. The pure white light continues to wash all over you. You feel fully present in the moment and realize that you and your guardian angel are experiencing perfect mindfulness together. You're no longer worried about any concerns from the past or future. You feel blessed, and time seems to stand still as you focus solely on

the present moment in the company of your guardian angel.

9. You feel a strong desire to pray, and so you thank the Divine for all the blessings in your life. You list some of the things you're grateful for, such as the gift of life, the protection and guidance of your guardian angel, the love of family and friends, and the ability to use your skills to help make the world a better place. You ask for healing so that you can continue to grow in this lifetime. You can pray to the Divine for as long as you wish. Finish by offering your gratitude and thanks.

10. Your guardian angel takes your hand, and together you ascend upward inside the column of pure white light. When you stop, you look down and see yourself sitting on the chair inside the column of pure white light. You know that your soul is looking down on your physical body. Surrounding you are the four great archangels, Raphael, Michael, Gabriel, and Uriel. You notice that Raphael, the archangel of healing, is looking at you. He has a huge smile on his face as he makes eye contact. You feel a flash of energy and know that Raphael will do everything he can to help you.

11. Your guardian angel squeezes your hand and you descend again. You don't want the ritual to end but realize it has when your angel gently releases your hand. "Thank you very much," you say. "I'm so grateful to have you in my life."

12. Sit quietly for a few moments. When you feel ready, stand up and say thank you and goodbye to the four great archangels.

13. Sit down once more and slowly count from one to five before opening your eyes.

14. Spend a few minutes thinking about what you experienced. Then, have something to eat and drink before returning to your everyday life.

You can repeat this ritual as often as you wish.

YOUR SPIRITUAL HEALTH

Your spiritual health is just as important as your physical and emotional health. When you're spiritually healthy, you'll feel a strong connection to a higher power and will be relaxed and at ease when communicating with the spiritual realms.

Auras

The aura is an electromagnetic energy field that surrounds the bodies of all living things. As the aura is also part of every cell in the body, it is actually an extension of the body, rather than something that surrounds it. The word "aura" comes from the Greek word *avra*, which means "breeze," an idea that references the energies that flow through our auras and reflect our personalities, thoughts, and emotions. Auras reveal a person's spiritual, mental, and physical well-being. Long-standing thoughts and emotions are seen in the aura, and if the person changes these long-held beliefs and emotions, the aura will change to reflect that. How you're feeling about life at any given moment is clearly visible to anyone who can read auras.

The human aura is roughly egg-shaped and extends eight to ten feet away from the body in all directions. Some highly spiritual people are said to have auras that extend for several miles, and their followers enjoyed spending time in their company partly because they could sense they were enfolded in their guru's aura. Gautama Buddha's early followers said that his aura extended two hundred miles (Eason, 11).

The aura expands and contracts depending on the person's health and vitality. Someone who is enthusiastic, energetic, and physically fit will have a much larger aura than someone who is negative and weak. The person with the larger aura will feel more in control of their life than the person with the smaller aura.

Auras contain all the colors of the spectrum. They can also change color depending on the person's feelings and emotions. Expressions such as "red with rage," "green with envy," and "feeling blue," all came about because people were able to see colors in people's auras.

When people first start to see auras, they appear to be white and almost cloudlike. With practice, the colors gradually become visible. Every aura has a basic color that reveals the person's emotional, mental, and spiritual nature. As well as this, the aura contains rays of different colors that emanate outward from the body.

The aura is not present when a baby is born but starts to appear as soon as the baby takes its first breath (Roberts, 7). This appears to indicate that the aura consists of energy that is absorbed into the body by the breath and radiated out again as the aura.

The aura is initially almost colorless but gains a silvery hue by the time the baby is about three months old. The silver color gradually changes to blue, indicating the development of intelligence. This usually happens between the ages of one and two. Simultaneously, a yellow haze appears around the head, revealing the start of thought. This haze becomes brighter and more powerful as the child continues to grow mentally. The aura gradually starts to reveal the child's potentials, and permanent colors start to appear, becoming obvious by the time the child starts school. The blue remains as a background color that can be seen only when the child is unwell. Over time, this blue diminishes and finally disappears.

The colors of the aura are powerful, pulsating, luminous vibrations of energy created by the electromagnetic charge of the aura. The frequency level of this light is slightly beyond the range of human eyesight, but it can be photographed and most people can learn to see it.

Every aura contains all the colors of the rainbow—red, orange, yellow, green, blue, indigo, and violet. These appear in the chakras, which we'll look at next. However, these and other colors can appear as a main color (often called the ground color), or as a radiating color inside the body of the aura. Here are the meanings of the main ground colors:

Red

Red denotes leadership potential and is always a powerful color. People with this color have strong egos and a desire to achieve success. This color is often subdued in childhood and only reaches its full potential when the people with it learn to stand on their own two feet and become independent.

Orange

Orange is a warm and caring color that is found in the auras of people who are intuitive, tactful, and easy to get along with. They are thoughtful, practical people who keep their feet firmly on the ground.

Yellow

People with yellow ground colors are excitable, enthusiastic, and changeable. They are gregarious, sociable people who love lengthy conversations with others. They are curious and enjoy learning but usually prefer to know a little bit about many topics as opposed to learning a great deal about one.

Green

Green is a peaceful color, and people with this as their ground color are peace-loving, co-operative, honest, and generous. They are natural healers. They appear calm and placid but can be highly stubborn when they feel it's necessary.

Blue

People with blue ground colors are naturally positive and enthusiastic. Despite having as many ups and downs as anyone else, this enthusiasm keeps them going and they always remain young at heart. They are sincere, generous, and usually speak their mind.

Indigo

Indigo is a soothing, healing, and nurturing color; people with it as a ground color usually choose humanitarian-type occupations. They enjoy helping others and are happiest when in the company of the people they love. They enjoy being responsible for others.

Violet

People with violet as their ground color grow inwardly and spiritually all the way through their lives. Many people with this ground color try to deny this quality and find life difficult until they embrace the spiritual side of their natures.

When people first start seeing auras, they usually see an almost clear space between the physical body and the aura. This is called the etheric double, and it expands while the person is asleep and contracts when they are awake. The etheric double seems to be a type of battery that recharges itself overnight. As a person gains aura consciousness, they can see that the etheric double is actually grayish in color and constantly shimmers, moves, and sometimes changes into a wide variety of delicate colors that constantly change.

The etheric double is sometimes called the health aura, as illnesses can be readily seen in it. Medical intuitives can often see signs of disease well before the person knows that there is a problem. This can be extremely useful information, as these people can take steps to restore their health before the situation becomes serious.

In addition to the etheric double, the aura consists of several layers that are called subtle bodies. Sometimes the colors of these vary. Clairvoyants usually see the aura as the etheric double, surrounded by a single layer with a variety of colors inside it. However, most people can learn to feel at least three of the subtle bodies, and healers and highly intuitive people can often feel the other layers, even if they can't see them. There are seven layers:

1. The physical etheric plane
2. The astral plane
3. The lower mental plane
4. The higher mental plane
5. The spiritual plane
6. The intuitional plane
7. The absolute plane

These seven layers relate to the seven chakras, the energy centers located alongside the spinal column inside the aura.

Chakras

The word *chakra* comes from the Sanskrit word for "wheel." Chakras are revolving, wheel-like circles of subtle energy inside the aura. They absorb higher energies and change them into a form that the body can use. Consequently, they play a vital role in a person's physical, mental, and emotional health. The seven main chakras are situated at different places along the spine and act as powerful batteries that energize the entire body. Each chakra is related to a physical system and the organs associated with it. Whenever a chakra is closed, blocked, or out of balance, it has an immediate effect on the health of the organs it is connected to. Any changes that restore and balance the chakra have an immediate positive effect on the body. As stress, frustration, and anger all affect the chakras, it's rare to find anyone with all seven chakras open and in balance.

Your guardian angel can help you keep your chakras well-balanced to ensure you lead a good life and progress as much as possible in this incarnation.

Root Chakra

Sometimes called the base chakra, the root chakra is situated at the base of the spine in the area of the coccyx. It keeps people firmly grounded to the earth. This chakra is concerned with self-preservation and provides feelings of security, vitality, energy, and comfort. It controls our fight-or-flight responses. It provides strength, courage and persistence, and symbolizes survival and the life force. At a physical level, the root chakra looks after the sense of smell, and the solid parts of the body, such as bones, teeth, and nails.

When the root chakra is understimulated, the person will feel insecure and nervous. When overstimulated, the person will be self-centered, overbearing, and addicted to power, money, and sexual gratification.

Call on your guardian angel to help you clear any energetic blocks to restore your root chakra if you feel fearful, anxious, and negative. Your guardian angel will also help you become fully grounded to the earth. On rare occasions and only when necessary, your guardian angel will call on Uriel, the archangel of the earth, for additional help.

Sacral Chakra

The sacral chakra is situated in the lower abdomen, approximately two inches below the navel. This chakra represents creativity, emotional balance, and sexuality. It stimulates hope, optimism, and positivity. It also relates to the sense of taste. When the sacral chakra is well-balanced, the person will relate easily to others.

When the sacral chakra is understimulated, the person is likely to suffer from arthritis, urinary problems, or sexual dysfunction, all accompanied by a loss of personal power. When overstimulated, the person will be aggressive, unscrupulous, and overly self-indulgent.

You can call on your guardian angel to restore your sacral chakra if you need help to gain more trust in yourself and your abilities. Your angel will also help you to eliminate negative energies that you no longer need. The more you believe in yourself, the more creativity and love will flow through your body, mind, and soul.

Solar Plexus Chakra

The solar plexus chakra is situated between the navel and the sternum. It provides personal power, confidence, warmth, happiness, and self-worth. It also relates to good digestion and a sense of physical well-being. It also relates to the eyes, which is not surprising, as everything seems brighter when we are feeling contented and happy. At an emotional level, the solar plexus chakra enhances creativity, trust, confidence, positivity, and self-respect. However, if the person has a negative approach to life, feelings of anger, hostility, and aggression are likely to build up.

When the solar plexus chakra is understimulated, the person will feel they are lacking control over what is going on in their life. When overstimulated, the person will be an overly demanding, humorless, perfectionist workaholic.

Call on your guardian angel to help you remain positive, calm, and sympathetic in all types of situations. Your guardian angel will work on your solar plexus chakra to help you gain inner peace, tranquility, wisdom, and understanding.

Heart Chakra
The heart chakra is in the center of the chest in line with the heart. It relates to all types of love, sympathetic understanding, empathy, healing, and the sense of touch. It enhances compassion, self-acceptance, and respect for everyone. If this chakra is well-balanced, the person will be nurturing, encouraging, and in touch with their feelings.

If the heart chakra is understimulated, the person will be overly sensitive, overly sympathetic, and feel afraid and sorry for themselves. Most codependents have understimulated heart chakras. When this chakra is overstimulated, the person will be possessive, selfish, controlling, and moody.

You can ask your guardian angel to work on your heart chakra and fill it with love and light, as well as to enable you to love and respect yourself. Your angel will help you restore harmony and peace whenever there is discord in your life.

Throat Chakra

The throat chakra is situated in the neck at the level of the throat. It relates to self-expression and communication, especially verbal communication. It seeks the truth and enhances idealism, understanding, and love. When the throat chakra is balanced, the person will be contented, enjoy peace of mind, have strong faith, and be kind and considerate to others.

When the throat chakra is understimulated, the person will be fearful, weak, unreliable, reserved, and withdrawn. When overstimulated, the person will be egotistical, inflexible, domineering, and sarcastic.

Call on your guardian angel to help you speak your truth by working on your throat chakra. Your angel will help you remove doubts and fears, choose your words carefully, be kind and gentle with the people you encounter, and to avoid gossip and any unwarranted criticism.

Brow Chakra

The brow or third eye chakra is situated in the forehead just above the eyebrows. This chakra is concerned with psychic and spiritual matters. It controls the mind and looks after the other chakras. At an emotional level, it makes people aware of their spiritual natures and enables them to pick up the thoughts, feelings, and even intuitions of others.

When the brow chakra is understimulated, the person will be nervous, diffident, non-assertive, and prone to tension headaches. When overstimulated, the person will be self-satisfied, authoritative, controlling, and inflexible.

Call on your guardian angel to work on your brow chakra to enable you to develop your spiritual and intuitive gifts for the benefit of all humanity. Your angel will help you forgive others and experience peace and contentment.

Crown Chakra

The crown chakra is situated at the top of the head. Artists often paint the crown chakra as a halo around the heads of people who are spiritually evolved. The crown chakra stabilizes and harmonizes the often-conflicting sides of our natures. It enables people to gain spiritual insight and understand the interconnectedness of all living things. The crown chakra can't be activated until all the other chakras are in a state of balance. When balanced, the person will experience enlightenment and gain a sense of being at one with the whole universe.

When the crown chakra is understimulated, the person will be taciturn, reserved, and unable to experience the joys of life. When overstimulated, the person will feel unfulfilled, and depressed, critical, and destructive. They will be likely to suffer from migraine headaches.

Ask your guardian angel to work on your crown chakra to bring clarity, understanding, inspiration, and positivity to your thoughts. You can also ask them to help you receive love, wisdom, understanding, and communication from the Divine.

HOW TO BALANCE YOUR CHAKRAS WITH YOUR GUARDIAN ANGEL

In chapter 3 we discussed using a pendulum to establish contact with your guardian angel. You can use the same pendulum to release any negativity in your chakras. All you need is your pendulum, a pen and paper, a glass, and a supply of water.

1. Suspend your pendulum, and ask it if your root chakra is in good health. If the answer is positive, you can move on and ask the same question about your sacral chakra. If the answer is negative, write this down on your sheet of paper. Continue asking this same question about each of the chakras in turn, recording a list of the names of the chakras which are out of balance.

2. Once you've assessed all seven chakras, you need to determine which of the chakras that gave a "no" answer is the most negative. Hold your pendulum over the name of each of the chakras on your sheet of paper in turn, and ask if that chakra is the most negative. Record the result and continue asking questions until you have established the order of negativity of the negative chakras.

3. Before going any further, ask your pendulum two questions: "Which movement indicates negative energies?" and "Which movement indicates positive energies?" Once you've done that, fill a glass with water.

4. Lay your pendulum down, close your eyes, and ask your guardian angel to join you, as you need to harmonize and balance your chakras. Open your eyes and say "thank you" once you sense your angel's presence.

5. Pick up your pendulum, and place the fingers of your other hand into the glass of water. Suspend the pendulum over the name of the most negative chakra, and ask it to remove all the negativity from this chakra. The pendulum will start moving in the direction that indicates negative energies. This is a sign that your guardian angel and your pendulum are removing all

the negativity from the affected chakra. Visualize the negativity coming up the pendulum, into your hand and arm, across your chest, and down your other arm into the glass of water. Take your fingers out of the water when the pendulum stops moving in the negative direction. Wash both of your hands under running water. Empty the glass of water, and give it a good wash before filling it again.

6. Repeat step five with the second most-afflicted chakra, and continue the process until all the chakras with negativity have been treated.

7. Now repeat step one to make sure that the negativity has been removed from all the afflicted chakras and they are now in balance. Sometimes you'll find that not all of the negativity has gone and you'll need to repeat the process of removing it (starting from step five). The chakras are not in balance until all seven give you a positive result.

8. The final step is to ask your guardian angel to fill every cell of your body with healing energy. Suspend your pendulum in front of you and close your eyes while your guardian angel does this. As green is considered a healing color, I visualize my guardian angel filling me, and the room I'm in, with pure green energy. It makes no difference what you visualize, as long as you sense that your guardian angel is filling you with positive healing energy. When you feel ready to open your eyes, ask your pendulum if your chakras are restored to their normal vibrant, healthy state. Pause for about ten seconds and then open your eyes. Your pendulum will

be moving in its positive direction to let you know that the chakra balancing was successful.

9. Thank your guardian angel for helping you to restore your chakras, and discuss anything you wish with your angel. Say "thank you" again and continue with your day.

After the chakra balancing, you should feel revitalized and full of energy. Some people feel emotional afterwards, which is not surprising, as emotional factors are often behind blockages in the chakras.

- Root: Insecurity, self-doubt, hanging on to difficulties from the past
- Sacral: Self-centeredness, selfishness, difficulties in communicating effectively with others
- Solar plexus: Low self-esteem, feelings of powerlessness and hopelessness
- Heart: Problems in expressing emotions, lack of empathy and compassion
- Throat: Frustration, inability to express innermost feelings
- Brow: Inability to accept the world as it is; spending most of the time in an unrealistic fantasy world
- Crown: Inflexibility, stubbornness, and isolation from others

If you're feeling worried and concerned about your health, contact your doctor. Some people find it hard to balance their own chakras because their health concerns can override the movements of the pendulum. If you experience this, ask someone else to balance your chakras for you. You can use the same method given earlier to balance someone else's chakras. Start by asking your guardian angel to ask the other person's guardian angel if they're happy for the chakra balancing to take place. I can't recall a single instance when permission has not been granted, but it's important to ask anyway. Assuming you've had a positive response, ask the person to lie down, so you can suspend your pendulum over each of their chakras in turn and bring the person's chakras back into balance.

HOW TO HARMONIZE YOUR CHAKRAS

The following is another method to harmonize and balance your chakras using your pendulum. As it can be done in a matter of minutes, it's a useful exercise to start the day with.

Copy the text below onto a sheet of paper or cardboard. You can modify or change the script if you wish, to make it suitable for your needs. I had mine laminated for protection, as I perform this brief ritual every day. Ask your guardian angel to bless the ritual. Hold your pendulum over the sheet of paper and allow it to swing in a clockwise direction as you read or say the words of the script.

"I ask the Universal Life Force and the angels to guard and protect me all day, no matter what I do or where I go. I ask for your protection at home, at work, and while I am traveling from place to place. I ask that honesty, integrity, and harmony be part of everything I'm involved in today, and that I retain a positive outlook in every situation I find myself within.

"I also ask that my chakra system remain in perfect balance and harmony throughout the day and help me act in every situation for the highest good of everyone involved.

"I ask that my activities today benefit everyone I come into contact with and that my aura remain bright, vibrant, and full of energy throughout the day.

"I allow my pendulum to continue making clockwise circles until my chakras are balanced; all negativity has been released from my body; and all fear, doubt, and worry have faded away and disappeared. Thank you, Universal Life Force and all the angels, including my guardian angel, for all the blessings in my life."

Once you've finished reading the script, continue holding your pendulum until it stops or changes direction. It's important that you do not stop as soon as you've finished saying the words, as it can take time for the ideas to be accepted. Once your pendulum stops or changes direction, thank it, and carry on with your day.

HOW TO SPREAD LOVE WITH YOUR GUARDIAN ANGEL

This is a useful exercise you can use to send love to a particular person, a group of people, or even to the whole world. You might like to send love to people who are sick in the hospital or to people working in dangerous occupations. You could send love to your work colleagues. Think also about sending love to people you don't like, to pets and other animals, and even the plants in your garden. There's no limit to where you can send your love.

I like to do this outdoors on a pleasant day. Whenever possible, I choose an attractive place where I'm unlikely to be interrupted. When this isn't possible, I find it just as effective to perform it indoors.

1. Stand with your legs slightly apart and with your arms loosely by your sides. Take three slow, deep breaths,

holding each inhalation for a few seconds before exhaling slowly.

2. Close your eyes. In your mind's eye, visualize yourself as clearly as possible. Once you've done that, visualize colors radiating from all seven of your chakras.

3. Focus on your root chakra at the base of your spine and ask your guardian angel to help you become fully grounded to the earth. "See" a powerful stream of energy radiating downward into the ground beneath you as your angel establishes a connection. You know that it's continuing deep into the earth, giving you a strong sense of confidence as you realize that you're fully grounded.

4. When you've visualized this powerful connection connecting you to the earth, turn your attention to your crown chakra at the top of your head. Ask your guardian angel to connect you with divine energy. Almost immediately, you "see" a pool of limitless energy floating in the air about two feet above your crown chakra. As you watch, energy pours downward from this pool and fills your crown chakra with divine energy.

5. Ask your guardian angel to fill each of your chakras with radiant energy, and smile as you "see" each chakra start to glow with incredible brilliance.

6. Now that you're fully grounded, have established a connection to the Divine, and charged your chakras, ask your guardian angel to help you send love to whomever you wish.

7. Your whole body seems to light up as you start radiating pure love in all directions. In your mind's eye you

see yourself as a tall, colorful beacon that continually gains energy as it sends love outward. You and your guardian angel might laugh with joy as you continue to radiate love from all of your chakras.

8. When you feel it is time to stop, thank your guardian angel, and watch as the outward radiations slow down. Once again you're able to see yourself in your mind's eye as you were before you started the exercise.

9. Thank your guardian angel once more and say good-bye. When you feel ready, take three slow, deep breaths and open your eyes.

With practice, you'll find that you can perform this ritual quickly and easily wherever you happen to be. For instance, you might read an article about the deforestation of the Amazon rainforest, and with the help of your guardian angel, instantly send love and healing to it.

SPIRITUAL GROWTH WITH YOUR GUARDIAN ANGEL

Spirituality has always been hard to define. Basically, it is the belief that humans possess a soul and are intimately connected to the Divine. Over the last fifty years, the phrase "spiritual but not religious" has become popular, showing that more and more people are finding their own spiritual path to the Divine.

Spiritual growth involves opening your mind and becoming aware that you are part of the Divine. It means that your soul is an inseparable part of the Divine and that you are a spirit who happens to currently live within a body. You are not simply a body, mind, and ego but something so much bigger and grander than any of these things. You are an immortal soul. You're also part of the same universal mind that gives life to all plants, creatures, and humankind.

The material world is also important; it's where we currently live. The purpose of this incarnation is to gain knowledge and wisdom, develop our talents and skills as much as we can, and to work on qualities that will benefit our soul, such as honesty, love, and humility. To achieve this, we need the help of the spiritual world.

Your guardian angel wants to help you embark on a journey of self-discovery and develop spiritually. Doing this will make you more compassionate and understanding. You'll become more loving and sympathetic. You'll gain peace of mind. Your life will be full of meaning and purpose. You'll gain a closer connection with the Divine. There are many ways to develop spiritually.

1. Reading books by people who are further ahead on this journey will give you plenty to think about. Discuss what you've read with your guardian angel.

2. Learning how to meditate will give you access to peace and quiet on a regular basis.

3. Praying regularly. Most prayers are petitionary prayers in which the person asks the Divine for help or for some other benefit. Contemplative prayers, often called "prayers of the heart," involve waiting quietly and listening for messages from the Divine. It is actually a combination of prayer and meditation.

4. Leading your life as positively as possible. This involves being honest, loving, patient, tolerant, understanding, and forgiving.

5. Taking control of your thoughts and feelings. Whenever you find yourself thinking negative thoughts, switch them around and replace them with positive

ones. The Scottish-Canadian philosopher Sydney Banks (1931–2009) said that at any given moment, we're all only one thought away from being happy or sad.

As you grow and progress spiritually, you'll learn a great deal of information that will be new to you. Hopefully most of it will be useful, but some may be misleading or negative. Some may even encourage you to go in the wrong direction or hold you back from following your true purpose. As this false information can come from anywhere, you need to be careful. Fortunately, you can ask your guardian angel if any information you receive is beneficial for you. I usually ask: "Is this information in harmony with my highest good?" Your guardian angel will give you a yes or no answer along with a reason for that particular response.

THREE BREATHS EXERCISE

This simple exercise can be done in a matter of seconds, and can be done anywhere, at any time. All you need do is to stop whatever it is you're doing, ask your guardian angel to join you, and take three slow breaths. Think a positive thought or affirmation for each breath. You might, for instance, say to yourself, "I am positive and happy" with the first breath, "I am peaceful and calm" on the second breath, and "I forgive myself and everyone who has ever hurt me" on the third. Thank your guardian angel and carry on with whatever you're doing.

Whenever possible, close your eyes while doing the Three Breaths exercise. You'll be pleasantly surprised at the difference a few slow, deliberate breaths accompanied by positive thoughts can make in your life.

THOUGHTFUL OBSERVATION

Dictionaries define contemplation as "thoughtful observation." For thousands of years, people have used contemplation to gain wisdom and to gain a closer connection with the Divine. Contemplation is not quite the same as thinking; while you're contemplating, your mind is quiet and relaxed, and in this meditative state you're able to observe, reflect, and ponder something. Because contemplation draws on your emotions and intuition as well as your mind, it can give you access to information you'd never be able to gain in any other way. Contemplation can help you learn what your heart and soul are trying to tell you.

You can use contemplation to provide answers to all sorts of questions. You can ask simple questions such as, "What can I do to make today a wonderful day?" You can also ask much more difficult questions, such as, "Should I persevere with my difficult marriage?"

You can also use contemplation to develop spiritually. It's an excellent way to study spiritual texts, as it enables you to fully comprehend and appreciate what the writer has to say. You can contemplate a single sentence or an entire book, depending on the amount of time you have at your disposal. The best way to start is to choose a short quote on angels, spirituality, or the soul. You might find the perfect phrase by chance. Alternatively, you can find them in books or on the Internet. Here are a few examples:

"You don't have a soul. You are a soul. You have a body."—C. S. Lewis (1898–1963), *Mere Christianity*

"Then cherish pity, lest you drive an angel from your door."—William Blake (1757–1827), *Holy Thursday*

"Be not forgetful to entertain strangers: for thereby some have entertained angels unawares."—Hebrews 13:2

"For he shall give his angels charge over thee, to keep thee in all thy ways."—Psalm 91:11

"Good thoughts will produce good actions and bad thoughts will produce bad actions. Hatred does not cease by hatred at any time; hatred ceases by love."—Buddha

With silence only as their benediction

God's angels come

Where, in the shadow of a great affliction,

The soul sits dumb.

> —James Greenleaf Whittier (1807–1892), from a letter to a friend whose sister had died.

SPIRITUAL CONTEMPLATION EXERCISE

1. Start by choosing a brief sentence or quote that appeals to you.

2. Sit down in a comfortable chair, and ask your guardian angel to help you with this contemplation exercise.

3. Read the passage that you've chosen, and close your eyes. Take three slow, deep breaths and allow your body to relax.

4. Open your eyes and read the passage again. Close your eyes and allow the words you've just read to filter through every cell of your body. Pay attention to your physical body and become aware of the effects these words have, especially in your heart and throat. Become aware of any sensations you might experience in your chakras. Ask your guardian angel to help you determine all the effects the words are having on your body, mind, and spirit.

5. Think about the words you've just read and ask: "What do they mean to me?" Take as long as you need to ponder the words.

6. If necessary, open your eyes and read the words again. Once you've done that, close your eyes, take another three slow, deep breaths, and again ask what the words mean to you. You can repeat this stage as many times as you wish.

7. When you feel you've absorbed all the knowledge you can from the words, thank your guardian angel for helping you, and slowly count from one to five and open your eyes.

8. As soon as possible after you've performed this exercise, write down all the thoughts and insights that came to you while you were contemplating.

I've met a few people who experienced good results with spiritual contemplation the very first time they tried it. I wasn't that fortunate; it took me several months to start having good results. Don't give up if you find it frustrating or difficult when you first experiment with it, as it will answer many of your spiritual questions and help your spiritual growth.

THE GUARDIAN ANGEL
BAGGAGE RELEASE RITUAL

We all carry baggage from the past with us, everywhere we go. Some people carry much more than others. An acquaintance of mine spends half her life apologizing, as she feels guilty about virtually everything. Here are some questions to ask yourself that will give you some idea of the amount of negative, emotional baggage you're currently carrying.

- Do you have any regrets?
- Do you endlessly think about your mistakes?
- Do you have fears, doubts, and worries?
- Do you ever feel like a victim?
- Do you take criticism personally?
- Do you have feelings of guilt?
- Do you constantly relive moments when someone said or did something unkind or hurtful to you?

If so, you'll find this baggage release ritual helpful and freeing.

These questions reveal just a few examples of the emotional baggage that everybody carries around with them. It's caused by how you feel about experiences that occurred in the past. This baggage can be crippling, drains self-esteem and energy, and makes it that much harder to fulfill your dreams. Emotional baggage can even cause physical pain. Wouldn't it be wonderful to let go of all these negative emotions and start living a successful and happy life? With the help of your guardian angel, you can.

This ritual can be performed in a few minutes anywhere you happen to be. As we all create new baggage for ourselves on a regular basis, it's wonderful to be able to perform this ritual frequently. Although I frequently perform a quick version of the ritual, I prefer to spend about twenty minutes performing this ritual whenever it's possible, starting with the Angelic Invocation of Protection. This means that I'm surrounded and protected by the four great archangels while I eliminate all the unwanted baggage. I recommend you do it this way too, especially when you first start performing this ritual. Once you've become familiar with it, you'll find you can close your eyes and perform the ritual whenever you have a few minutes to spare.

1. Create a magic circle, and start by performing the Angelic Invocation of Protection in chapter 3.

2. Sit down comfortably in a straight-backed chair in the center of your magic circle. Make sure the room is pleasantly warm. It's hard to perform a ritual when you're uncomfortably cold or if you're perspiring when the temperature is too high.

3. In your mind's eye, visualize yourself sitting comfortably with your eyes closed. Take three slow, deep breaths, and then consciously relax all the muscles in your body, from the tips of your toes to the top of your head. Once you've done that, mentally scan your body to make sure that you're completely relaxed. Focus on any areas that have not yet relaxed completely until they let go.

4. Once you've confirmed that you're completely relaxed, ask your guardian angel to help you release all the baggage that's holding you back. Your guardian angel is with you always, and you'll be able to sense this when you talk directly to your angel. Sense your angel's presence, and in your imagination, extend an arm. Sense your angel taking hold of it and giving it a gentle tug. You might "see" your guardian angel in your mind's eye. When you feel the tugging motion, visualize your guardian angel pulling you gently up into the air. It's a wonderful feeling, as if you're floating on air. To your surprise, you pass right through the roof of the building you're in and start ascending up, up, up into the air.

You stop moving when your angel lets go of your arm and relax even more as you enjoy the feeling of floating gently in midair.

5. Your guardian angel telepathically tells you that you need to visualize yourself as you are now, and to then imagine yourself gradually changing shape and morphing into a huge ball of wool. You feel a sense of excitement as you experience this happening. You are now a large ball of wool floating in the sky.

6. Your guardian angel tells you to notice that the ball is not smooth and round, as there are strands of wool spooling off in every direction. Your angel tells you that each strand is attached to a piece of emotional baggage you're carrying around with you.

7. While you're visualizing yourself as a huge ball of wool floating in space, your guardian angel shows you a large pair of scissors and tells you they are going cut off all the strands of wool so that the ball of wool will be almost perfectly round, although it may not be completely round. Your angel won't cut off any baggage that relates to your immediate family because these are karmic matters you'll have to work through yourself.

8. Your guardian angel waits a few moments to make sure that you understand what's going to happen and then starts cutting off strands of wool. It happens at lightning speed, and you can scarcely see the scissors move as it cuts strands of wool, releasing more and more emotional baggage with each cut. Your guardian angel circles around you several times until you've become an almost completely round and smooth ball of wool.

9. Your guardian angel continues to circle you and makes sure that all the unwanted baggage has been released. Once satisfied, your angel tells you that you're turning back into your normal, everyday self, but that you'll be lighter than before, as you've lost all the baggage that was weighing you down.

10. Sense yourself gradually returning to your normal size and shape. Even though you're floating in the air, you can sense how much lighter and happier you are. After a few moments, your guardian angel takes hold of your arm again and you start descending back to your comfortable chair on the ground. It's such a peaceful and relaxing feeling that you feel you could simply continue floating forever. Your angel lets go of your arm once you're sitting comfortably in your chair again.

11. Visualize your guardian angel standing in front of you, asking you to forgive yourself for all the harm you have unintentionally caused yourself.

12. Your angel then tells you there's one final step that you may or may not want to do at this time. Are you willing to forgive everyone who has been responsible—knowingly or unknowingly—for the instigating moment that caused the emotional baggage to form? Your guardian angel suggests that you send unconditional love to everyone who has ever caused you pain or hurt. Your angel smiles gently and gives you enough time to think about this question and respond to it. Once you've answered the question, you sense your angel surrounding you with love. Say a sincere thank-you and goodbye

to your guardian angel. Although your guardian angel has finished the ritual, you know they are still with you.

13. Spend a minute or two quietly relaxing, and enjoying the feeling of lightness and happiness in your body. When you feel ready, count slowly from one to five, open your eyes, stretch, and stand up.

14. If you've performed the full ritual with the Angelic Invocation of Protection, thank the four great archangels and dismiss them one by one.

Don't rush back into your everyday life as soon as you've completed the ritual. Spend a few minutes thinking about what you've just achieved, and then eat and drink something. You'll then be ready to return to normal life again, feeling lighter and happier than you were before.

Because we all pick up unwanted baggage as we go through life, it's best to perform this ritual regularly.

Once you've eliminated your unwanted baggage, you'll find it helpful to work on any limiting beliefs you may have, too, as they often work together.

LIMITING BELIEFS

Everyone experiences difficulties as they progress through life. Even people who seem to go through life with few problems may have had to cope with financial difficulties, relationship problems, health setbacks, career frustrations, and other difficulties along the way. Some fortunate people are able to resolve their problems without too many complications. Most people, though, have an area of life that they constantly struggle with—no matter what they do and how hard they try, nothing seems to work.

These people are likely to have deep-seated subconscious beliefs that hold them back, limit their lives, and prevent them from enjoying the abundant and happy life they should be living. These limiting beliefs are thoughts and opinions that often date back to early childhood. Someone who grew up in a loving and supportive family will believe they are loved and wanted, while a child who is mistreated may develop a belief that they are unworthy, unwanted, and unlovable. For example, a child whose parents constantly said "Money doesn't grow on trees" and "We can't afford that" is likely to develop negative thoughts about money and success. All children pick up a number of beliefs in early childhood. Some will be positive and supportive, but others will have been developed as a protective mechanism to shield the person from pain.

Thoughts control emotions, and emotions control behavior in turn. For example, if you experienced a bad relationship breakup when you were young, you might start thinking negatively about relationships in general and subconsciously decide that all of your relationships will be painful and difficult. As you now believe that this is the case, you'll subconsciously cause it to become true. This shows the power of your thoughts, and how important it is to be kind to yourself.

Limiting beliefs are created in a number of ways other than from parents. They can come from the person's early life experiences or from societal standards and expectations that the person finds hard to live up to. They can be caused by a fear of failure at something the person's peers are able to do. The comments of authority figures such as parents, other family members, spiritual leaders, and others can create limiting beliefs. The comments of peer groups frequently lead to limiting beliefs. Religions play a major role in creating limiting beliefs, as the person might find it difficult to live up to the particular religion's attitudes and teachings.

Fortunately, it's possible to change limiting beliefs. When I was at high school, my French teacher told me that I was hopeless with languages. Because he was in a position of authority, I accepted what he said and believed that I would never learn foreign languages. More than thirty years later, I spent a week at the Frankfurt Book Fair in Germany. Because I spoke no German and my budget was limited, I had to eat at McDonald's, where I could simply point at the large menu when ordering my meals. When I decided to return to the book fair the following year, I was determined not to eat all my meals at McDonald's again. A few months before returning to Frankfurt, I bought some tapes and an introductory book on German. I found that learning a new language wasn't as difficult as I'd expected it to be. In fact, much to my surprise, I found I was good at learning a foreign language. My self-limiting belief about languages disappeared as soon as I realized it was wrong. With the help of my guardian angel, I've since eliminated other beliefs that were holding me back.

The first step is to find out what self-limiting beliefs you're holding on to. The most common ones relate to:

- Fear of rejection
- Fear of not being good enough
- Fear of failure
- Fear of success
- Fear of being unlovable
- Feeling unworthy
- Fears about money
- Fears about being too young or too old
- Fears about what other people might think

Before you can eliminate your limiting beliefs, you need to know what they are. Start by making a list of all your beliefs to determine which ones are helping you and which ones are holding you back. Include your beliefs about money, relationships, family, health, and career. Think about times when you let yourself down or behaved badly, and consider whether any beliefs might be behind them. Think about any personal challenges you have and ask yourself which beliefs are causing them.

No matter how many limiting beliefs you discover, work on changing one belief at a time. You might find that being aware of the unwanted belief is all that's required. Once you know what it is, you can recognize the harm it is doing to your life and create a new, positive belief to replace it. That's what I did with my belief about being hopeless at foreign languages. Once I discovered the belief served no purpose in my life and was holding me back, I was able to let it go and replace it with the new belief that I'm good at learning languages.

Although every limiting belief can be overcome, some are more complex than others. Fortunately, as you know, your guardian angel is ready and waiting to help you. Here's a guided visualization with your guardian angel that will help you eliminate any unwanted subconscious beliefs.

Set aside about thirty minutes of time when you know you won't be disturbed. Make sure the room is warm enough and you're wearing comfortable, loose-fitting clothes. You might like to play some relaxing New Age music too. I prefer silence, but everyone is different—do what works best for you.

1. Sit in a comfortable chair, close your eyes, and think about your guardian angel for a minute or two. Give thanks for everything your angel has done for you, and

say how much you're looking forward to receiving more help and advice in the future.

2. When you feel ready, inhale deeply to the count of three, hold your breath for a few seconds, and then exhale to the count of three. Take several of these slow, deep breaths and allow your body to relax more and more with each exhalation.

3. Now forget about your breathing and visualize yourself walking through an art museum. You have the entire museum to yourself and can stop and examine any paintings you wish. Soon you find yourself in a gallery full of landscapes. For some reason, you feel yourself attracted to one in particular, a beautiful scene that makes you feel happy and joyful just to look at it.

4. You move closer to examine the artist's brushstrokes and suddenly experience a strange sense that you're not just looking at the landscape, you're actually inside it. You turn around in a circle and find yourself standing right in the middle of the landscape. You feel a gentle breeze. As you look upward, you see fluffy clouds moving across the pure blue sky. You hear the song of a flight of birds as they fly in formation high up in the sky.

5. You start walking and feel the sun's warm rays on your back. Soon you find a path that takes you to a viewing platform, where you look down over a beautiful valley that wasn't visible in the painting. A stream runs through the middle of the valley, and you can see horses and cows grazing on the lush grass on both sides

of the stream. You can't see anyone, but you notice that the path continues downhill to the valley floor. Halfway down is a comfortable seat offering a perfect view of the valley and you walk down to it.

6. When you reach the seat and sit down, you feel a wave of relaxation pass through you as you look at the magnificent view. A cow moos, as if echoing your thoughts. You smile and feel more at peace than you've been for a long, long time. You enjoy these feelings as you look around and realize that this is the perfect place to have a conversation with your guardian angel.

7. You've no sooner thought this than you sense your guardian angel's presence. "Thank you for joining me," you say. "I need your help, as something has been holding me back for a long time, and I need your help to get rid of it." Tell your angel about the limiting belief you have and some of the negative things that have happened to you as a result of it. Explain that you know it's a belief and not a fact, but it's causing you pain and holding you back from being the person you want to be. Ask your guardian angel to help you eliminate it.

8. Listen quietly to what your angel has to say. Your angel is likely to sympathize with you, and will express pleasure that you're ready to discard anything holding you back from leading the life you could and should be enjoying.

9. Once your guardian angel has expressed their empathy, you sense that you're about to learn some good, practical information. Your angel starts by asking you to name two or three people, alive or dead, whom you

admire and look up to. After you've provided their names, your guardian angel asks you how these people would have handled the problem if they'd suffered from the same limiting belief.

10. After you've thought about that, your guardian angel asks you to think of something new you can do to replace the old, damaging, limiting belief. You have the ability to choose whatever you wish. It needs to be something positive, bold, and brave. Whatever it is will take time, courage, and persistence to achieve. It won't necessarily be easy. You might have a few setbacks before the new belief totally eliminates the old one and becomes a natural part of your life.

11. You sense the love, encouragement, and support of your guardian angel as you absorb what you've learned. Your angel asks you to visualize what your life will be like once you've changed. Will it be worth it? You decide that it will, and you feel how happy your guardian angel is with your reply. Your guardian angel tells you to focus on your skills, talents, and achievements. Most of all, your angel wants you to believe in yourself. You feel a tingling sensation in the area of your sacral chakra, two inches below your navel, as you hear this. You know this chakra relates to your most basic emotions, and you feel happy and proud that it's working exactly as it should be.

12. You thank your guardian angel for being there for you and for always being so willing to help. Your angel tells you to repeat the visualization as often as you wish until the limiting belief has completely gone.

13. You look at the quiet, peaceful scene in front of you for a minute or two before getting up and following the path back to where it began. In a moment, you find yourself at the location inside the painting where you started. You pause for a moment and then step directly into the gallery in the art museum. You look at the painting you traveled within, and when you feel ready, you count from one to five and open your eyes.

14. Sit quietly for a minute or two before getting up. Think about the wonderful experience you've had, and reflect on the help and advice you received from your guardian angel. Thank your angel once again for helping you resolve your problem. When you feel ready, get up. Have something to eat and drink, and continue with your day.

Repeat this visualization regularly until the limiting belief has gone. Think about the information and advice your guardian angel provided at least twice a day. Think about the people you admire, and ask yourself how they would deal with your problem. Whenever you have a spare moment, repeat the affirmation your guardian angel gave you: "I believe in myself."

As you and your guardian angel work together on eliminating your unwanted baggage and limiting beliefs, the quality of your life will steadily improve.

SELF-ESTEEM AND YOUR GUARDIAN ANGEL

Your guardian angel wants to help you become the very best you possible, which won't happen if you're lacking confidence and self-esteem. When you feel good about yourself, you're much more likely to be confident; you'll believe in yourself and will trust yourself and your abilities. You'll value yourself and feel happier. Self-esteem is the knowledge that you can handle whatever is going on in your life and that you have just as much a right to feel happy as anyone else.

Even if you feel you're lacking in confidence, you already have confidence in many areas of your life. You're confident that your heart will continue beating, for instance, and that your eyes will blink when necessary. You can become this level of confident in other situations too, as soon as you learn to feel differently in uncertain situations. This means that your subconscious mind will have learned new, more effective ways to deal with potentially difficult situations.

Here's a guided visualization exercise you can do with your guardian angel that will help you gain confidence and self-esteem. Before doing it, make two lists: one of the areas of life that you feel totally confident in, and the other listing areas where you need more confidence.

You can do this exercise in two different ways. You could record the script and listen to it when you're feeling relaxed. Alternatively, you could read it a few times to familiarize yourself with it and then silently direct yourself through it in your own words. There are benefits to both methods. A recorded script keeps you on track and ensures you receive all the necessary information. However, the disadvantage is that you may want to spend more time in one scene and less in another. You can make the session as long or as short as you wish when using your own words. You might, for instance, need more or less time to become fully relaxed. You can also change the script to suit you and your particular needs.

You need to allow about thirty minutes for this visualization. Wear loose-fitting clothes and make sure that the room you're in is pleasantly warm. Temporarily turn off your phone. Sit down in a comfortable chair, or lie down on a sofa or bed. I like to use a recliner-type chair, as I tend to fall asleep if I'm lying down on a bed. You might like to cover yourself with a rug or blanket, too. You should do anything else that makes you feel relaxed and comfortable.

When you're ready, play your recording or start telling yourself the script in your own words. Here is the script:

"Take a nice deep breath in, and close your eyes as you exhale. Let all those muscles relax. Each breath you take helps you relax more and more. It's so pleasant to simply relax and let all the cares of the day fade away, while you drift and float in this nice, calm, peaceful relaxed state.

"In your mind, see yourself standing at the top of a beautiful staircase. It's the most beautiful staircase you've ever seen, and you pause to admire it before going down the stairs. You notice the staircase has ten steps leading down to a magnificent garden full of colorful flowers. At the foot of the staircase is a large thickly-piled rug decorated with an intricate pattern, and you instantly know that it's a flying carpet that can magically transport you to any place you wish to visit.

"You place one hand on the banister and stand on the top step. 'Ten,' you say to yourself, and you feel a wave of relaxation pass through you as you exhale.

"You take another deep breath as you go down to the next step. 'Nine,' you silently say, as you double your relaxation.

"As you step down once more, you anticipate what's going to happen. 'Eight,' you say, and your relaxation doubles yet again.

"You are feeling so relaxed now, and you smile as you move down one more step. 'Seven,' you say to yourself, and your body relaxes even more.

"You move down one more step. You feel so relaxed that you feel you couldn't relax even more. Amazingly, you double your relaxation yet again as you say the word 'six.'

"You're halfway down the staircase now as you take one more step, and say 'five.'

"The magic carpet starts vibrating slightly as you look at it, and you feel excited as you realize that you'll soon be sitting on it. You take another step, and feel limp, loose, lazy, and so, so relaxed as you say, 'four.'

"You're so relaxed that it's almost too much effort to move now. However, as you want to feel totally calm and relaxed, you move down one more step, and say 'three.' Every cell of your body responds as you double your relaxation yet again.

"There are just two steps to go. You double your relaxation and feel totally, utterly, completely relaxed as you take one more step, and say, 'two.'

"You pause before taking the last step, feeling the anticipation and excitement building up inside you as you look at the flying carpet, which is now floating a few inches above the ground. It shakes slightly, as if encouraging you to take the last step. Every cell in your body is now more relaxed than ever before, and yet you double that relaxation as you descend the final step, and say, 'one.'

"The flying carpet rises up to meet you, and you smile as you step onto it. You plan to sit on the carpet, but it's too much effort. You lie down instead. You know that the carpet will react instantly to your thoughts and take you anywhere you want to go. You spend a few moments thinking about the places you'd like to visit. It might be a place you know well. It could be somewhere you've always wanted to go to. It might be an imaginary place where everything is perfect.

"Once you've made your decision, the magic carpet reads your thoughts. You're instantly high up in the air, traveling through time and space at breathtaking speed. You feel comfortable and thoroughly enjoy the ride. It's over far too quickly, and you look around with interest as the carpet slows down and gently descends to the ground.

"You step off your magic carpet and watch as it ascends upward again and quickly disappears from view. You start walking, and before long you find a beautiful place where you can sit and relax for as long as you wish. It's so peaceful, so quiet, and so relaxing. The temperature is perfect, the sky is cloudless, and the only sounds you hear are birds singing as they soar high above you.

"Now that you feel fully relaxed in this nice, calm, beautiful place, ask your guardian angel to join you. You may or may not see your guardian angel in your mind's eye, but you'll know your angel is there. After all, your angel is with you all day, every day. You know that your angel will be delighted to help you overcome any problems or issues you have in your life. As your angel wants you to be as happy and as fulfilled as possible, you know that you'll receive all the help you need to gain confidence and self-esteem. Smile and feel a sense of positivity throughout your entire body as you greet your guardian angel.

"Thank your guardian angel for joining you. Tell your angel how grateful you are, as you need more confidence and self-esteem. Say that you're willing to do whatever is necessary to improve because you know that it will help your life in so many ways.

"This is the time to tell your guardian angel the areas of life you're confident in, and the areas where you need help." (Pause the recording for about sixty seconds.)

"And now your guardian angel gives you valuable information that you accept wholeheartedly. Your angel speaks seriously, and tells you that from now on, no matter what happens in your life, you'll love yourself, respect yourself, and trust yourself. You'll no longer care what other people say or think. You are your own person, and you like yourself. Other people are attracted to you too, because you're confident, honest, caring, and empathic. You are a good friend. You trust your own judgment because you believe in yourself, and you're on the road to success.

"Your guardian angel continues: 'As each day passes, you'll become more relaxed in every type of situation. You'll speak to others easily. You'll feel at ease whenever you are with others, be it one person or a thousand. Words come easily, and you'll present yourself in a warm, confident manner. You're interested in other people and you focus on them and their needs. You'll no longer feel embarrassed or self-conscious.'

"Your guardian angel asks you to relive a scene from the past where you felt lacking in confidence and failed to reveal the real you. Visualize this scene on a small, old-fashioned black-and-white television screen." (Pause for about ten seconds.) "Good. And now rerun that scene again, but this time see yourself doing everything exactly the way you wished it had been. Sense the presence of your guardian angel supporting you this time. Watch this scene in radiant color on a huge cinema screen." (Pause for ten seconds.)

"Notice the difference. Look at the small black and white screen again and see how much smaller the screen has become. Look at the huge cinema screen and notice that it's now larger and the colors are even more vivid and beautiful. Switch from one screen to the other a few more times. Each time you do this, the black-and-white screen becomes smaller and the cinema screen grows larger and larger. Soon the black-and-white screen becomes so small that you can't see it, and the large colorful screen entirely surrounds you. It represents the new you. With the help of your guardian angel, you are the star of your own show. From now on, you'll be displaying the very best of yourself to the world.

"Your angel is telling you to let go of all the pain and heartache from the past. You watched all of that on the black-and-white screen but are now reliving these experiences the way they should have been, on the enormous cinema screen. It feels so good to be creating these new memories in the company of your guardian angel. You're excited to know that you can do this whenever you want to change a negative memory. All you need do is to switch back and forth between the two screens until the small screen disappears. Whatever was shown on that screen was worthless, nothing. It always was nothing, and now it's gone. You can do this exercise as often as you wish and whenever you wish.

"From now on you'll wake up every morning feeling confident and ready for any challenges life has for you. You have all the confidence you need in every type of situation. You feel worthy, valuable, and deserving of respect.

"And now it's time to ask your guardian angel any questions you wish about anything at all." (Pause for sixty seconds.)

"When you've finished asking questions, your guardian angel tells you to do something every day that makes you feel good about yourself. It can be anything at all, as long as it makes you feel positive, happy, and proud of your skills and abilities. Your angel tells you that it can be something small or large. The most important part is to do at least one positive thing every day to bolster your self-esteem.

"Feel your guardian angel surrounding you in a warm embrace. Smile and thank your special angel for all the good things in your life and for always being there for you. Your angel continues hugging you until you notice the flying carpet has returned and is hovering directly in front of you. 'Thank you,' you say to your guardian angel.

You step onto the flying carpet and sit down. There's just enough time to wave to your guardian angel and to say thank you and goodbye, before the carpet soars up into the air and in a matter of seconds takes you back home. You realize that the visualization is over, and you're lying down with your eyes closed, feeling relaxed and comfortable. You also feel positive about every aspect of your life.

"Enjoy the pleasant feelings of relaxation in your body for as long as you wish, and remember and relive parts of the visualization. When you feel ready, count slowly from one to five and open your eyes."

Sit quietly for a few minutes and enjoy the feelings of confidence inside. Thank your guardian angel once again, and have something to eat and drink before returning to your everyday life.

To achieve the best results, you should perform this visualization at least once a week until the problem has been resolved.

Your guardian angel is always with you, no matter what is happening in your life. Your angel wants to celebrate the good times with you, and is just as willing to provide help and consolation during difficult periods.

HOW TO MEND A BROKEN HEART

Heartbreak is one of the most devastating experiences anyone can have, and almost everyone suffers from it at some time during their lives. Broken hearts are usually associated with relationship breakups, but they can occur in other ways too. Many people have experienced it after the death of a partner, close friend, or a much-loved pet. A friend of mine had made a new life for himself in a different country, and it broke his heart when the government refused to extend his visa, forcing him to return to his country of birth. An acquaintance experienced a broken heart when what she considered to be her dream job came to an end and she was made redundant.

No matter the cause of the heartbreak, it's always accompanied by almost unbearable anguish and emotional pain. Fortunately, a broken heart can be healed. It takes time, as it always involves a grieving process. You need to be kind to yourself and allow yourself time to grieve. You need to take care of yourself, too: eat healthily, keep hydrated, and take regular exercise. Try to do something every day that makes you laugh. Watching a cartoon or a stand-up comedian releases endorphins which will make you feel good for a short while, and will help your mental and emotional health. Although unlikely to happen right away, the healing *will* happen.

Your guardian angel wants to help you with every step of the process. Sit down somewhere where you won't be disturbed and have a heart-to-heart conversation with your guardian angel about what happened and how you feel. It's good to express your emotions and feelings, especially when you're surrounded with the love and support of your guardian angel. Your angel is endlessly patient and will listen and make suggestions that will help you for as long as you wish. You can talk with your guardian angel whenever you want and as frequently as you wish.

This creative visualization will help you release some of the hurt and pain. You might like to record it and use the recording. However, for this particular visualization, it might be better to read it a few times and then say it to yourself with your eyes closed while doing the visualization. A recording may be too fast or slow for your particular needs at the time you do it. You will need about thirty minutes of uninterrupted time.

Before you start, prepare your surroundings. You'll need a comfortable chair to relax in; a recliner is ideal. The room needs to be comfortably warm, and you should wear loose-fitting clothes. If you wish, play some quiet relaxation music. Here is the script:

"Take a nice, deep breath in, hold it for a few moments, and close your eyes as you exhale. Be aware of yourself, sitting in your chair with your eyes closed, and know that you're in control. You're about to embark on a healing visualization with your guardian angel, and you feel comfortable. There's no rush. You don't need to hurry. Just enjoy the pleasant feelings of relaxation entering different parts of your body. All you need do is relax, and allow it to happen.

"You may hear sounds from outside the room. They don't bother or disturb you. In fact, they help you drift even deeper into relaxation. In a moment, you'll feel yourself drifting into a light and gentle trance-like state. It reminds you of the times when you almost fell asleep while watching television. You could hear what was being said but it washed over you, helping you to drift even deeper into a calm, gentle, relaxed state.

"Feel yourself drifting and floating, almost as if you were relaxing in a fluffy white cloud high up in the sky where nothing can bother or disturb you. You notice that other parts of your body are relaxing now, and you realize how beneficial it is for you to let go of all the stress, tension, and anxiety—to simply be. It's so good for you to relax and let life pass you by for a few moments.

"In your imagination, picture yourself now floating in your beautiful fluffy cloud, high above the world. You're floating in a beautiful blue sky, and from this vantage point you can see that it's possible to view things in quite a different way than before. As you're drifting along, you allow all the tension and stress in your body to dissolve and disappear. You don't need them anymore.

"You feel calm, safe, secure, and so, so relaxed. You can't be bothered with all the pain, hurt, and negativity that's been holding you back, and you consciously set it free. Enjoy the sensation of being free again—free and in control. Yes, you're in control, and you can prove this to yourself by directing your cloud higher or lower, or maybe changing direction.

"You're surrounded by health-giving, life-giving, pure, fresh air. It feels good to finally let go of all the negative feelings and emotions and simply relax in your beautiful cloud in the sky.

"There's only one person you want to speak with right now. That's right—it's your guardian angel. Your special angel has been with you all along, and you can feel the special warmth and love of your guardian angel all around you.

"You smile and greet your guardian angel. 'I should have known that you were here with me,' you say. 'I am always with you,' your angel replies. 'Today, I'm here to help you heal your broken heart. I sense that the time is right and you're ready. How do you feel about that? Is it time?' 'Yes,' you reply. 'I'm more than ready. Thank you.'

"'Good,' your guardian angel says. 'First, we have to return you to your chair.' You start to answer, but before you can get a single word out, you realize that you're no longer floating in the sky but sitting in your recliner chair inside your room. 'We're now going to fill you with healing energy,' your angel says. 'Not only that, I have healing angels here with me, and they're going to heal your heart.'

"You sense a pure white stream of light descending from the heavens and entering your body through the top of your head. You feel a wave of exhilaration and delight. You look upward and see the ray of light. Inside it are hundreds of tiny, smiling angels. You can hear their laughter as they float downward and into your body.

"Your guardian angel speaks again. 'In just a moment, the healing angels will start cleansing and healing your heart. No matter what condition your heart is in, they'll restore it.' You focus on your heart and feel a sense of comfort and warmth as the healing angels perform their work.

"'That's good,' your guardian angel says. 'The angels have repaired the outside of your heart. Now they'll go inside and see what needs to be repaired there.' You feel a sense of release inside your whole body. 'Just relax,' your angel says. 'The healing angels are releasing all the hurt, pain, anger, and any other unresolved issues from the past. Soon you'll be whole again.'

"Time seems to stop as the healing angels restore your heart. You can sense the stream of white light continuing to enter your body and feel a warmth in your heart. You also feel love in your heart and sense it growing and expanding well beyond your physical body. 'That's it,' says your guardian angel. 'You're free to love again. Look—you're sending your love out into the world.'

"'The healing angels have finished,' your guardian angel says. 'Look up.' You look up, and see the healing angels flying up the stream of light as they return to the Divine. They look happy, and some of them wave to you as they fly upward.

"'Thank you, healing angels,' you call out to them. 'I can't thank you enough.' You feel your heart filling with gratitude for all they've done for you. You watch until the last healing angel has flown up through the white light. The light gradually fades and disappears. 'Thank you very much, Guardian Angel,' you say. 'I'm so lucky having you to help me. I think I can start living again.' Your guardian angel laughs. 'You have a great deal to live for! You have so much happiness and love ahead of you. But remember: there could be a few ups and downs before you're completely on track. All you need do is ask, and we can call on the healing angels whenever you need them.' 'Thank you.' Your guardian angel laughs again and asks, 'Would you like to relax on your cloud for a while before you return to your normal life?' You reply that you would.

"Instantly, you find yourself high above the world, floating on your fluffy white cloud. You can enjoy the experience for as long as you wish. When it's time to return, you know that all you need do is count slowly from one to five, and open your eyes. 'Thank you, Guardian Angel,' you say again. 'Good night.'"

You can do this creative visualization as often as you wish until your heart is completely mended, and you're moving forward again.

HOW TO WORK WITH OTHER PEOPLE'S GUARDIAN ANGELS

Once you start working with your guardian angel, you'll discover just how much your angel wants to help you progress in life. Getting on with and helping other people are important parts of this. Your guardian angel will help you make friends, resolve difficulties with others, and send love and healing to people who need it.

HOW TO ASK YOUR GUARDIAN ANGEL TO SPEAK TO ANOTHER PERSON'S GUARDIAN ANGEL

We've already mentioned (chapter 1) how Pope Pius XI and Pope John XXIII asked their guardian angels to help whenever they were going to have a meeting with someone who could be difficult to deal with. Both asked their guardian angels to speak with the other person's guardian angel and resolve any problems before the meeting began. You don't need to be a pope to do this. All you need do is to speak with your guardian angel ahead of time, explain why you want the meeting to be a success, and ask for help. Your guardian angel will talk with the other person's guardian angel, and discuss the areas of difficulty, which means you won't need to worry about them while you're talking with the other person. Recently, I heard about a high school student who asked his guardian angel to talk to the guardian angel of a teacher who he felt didn't like him. He noticed a difference right away and is now doing well in this teacher's class.

You can ask your guardian angel to communicate with other people's guardian angels for any worthwhile purpose. If you've had a disagreement with a friend or family member, for instance, you can ask your guardian angel to help resolve the problem by discussing it with the other person's guardian angel.

HOW TO SEND HEALING TO OTHERS WITH YOUR GUARDIAN ANGEL

You can also ask your guardian angel to send love and healing to anyone you care to name. Your angel will also do this for groups of people, no matter how large they might be. Padre Pio is said to have regularly sent his guardian angel to give comfort and help to others (Ronner, 118).

All you need do is to sit quietly somewhere where you won't be disturbed. Close your eyes, relax, and start talking with your guardian angel. During the conversation, tell your angel about the person you're concerned about, and ask for healing to be sent to this person. Your angel may or may not tell you what action will take place. They might refer the matter on to Archangel Raphael or any other healing angels. Your angel might communicate with the ill person's guardian angel and decide what course of treatment would be best. Once you've passed the matter on to your guardian angel, you can relax knowing that the angels will do the best they can to effect a healing. You can help the progress by praying and sending healing thoughts to the person who needs it.

FULL-COLOR GUARDIAN ANGELS

Some years after the death of Mechtilde Thaller (1868–1919), the remarkable German stigmatic and mystic, her notebooks were published. They proved extremely popular, as they described her relationship with her guardian angel and many other angels. Throughout her life, she was able to see angels, and from the age of five she was guided and supported by both her guardian angel and an archangel.

As a child, she is said to have prayed to God to heal the blindness of a young girl she saw begging in the street. She wiped the girl's eyes with her lace handkerchief, and the girl's sight was restored. This is just one of the many miracles she is said to have performed.

When she was a teenager, Father Schorra, her spiritual director, refused to let her enter into a religious life. He told her that God wanted her to be married. Unfortunately, the man she married was an adulterous tyrant who constantly abused her. They had no children, but Mechtilde had a large number of "spiritual children" she visited and exchanged letters with.

Mechtilde had the ability to bilocate, which meant she was able to be in two places simultaneously. During the First World War she used this talent to nurse wounded soldiers close to the front line. Her guardian angel told her to keep her gifts a secret. Remarkably, she was able to keep the fact that she had stigmata on her hands and body a secret from everyone except her spiritual director.

Throughout her life, Mechtilde was taught by angels, and she recorded all of the revelations she learned in her notebooks. Her writing included descriptions of different angels, information about the hierarchy of angels, and the job descriptions of angels in each rank. She said that the personalities of guardian angels varied enormously. Some were active and energetic, while others were more reserved and appeared shy and diffident. She wrote that the more reserved guardian angels looked after people who "are called to suffer much." Unfortunately, Mechtilde's diaries and notebooks have not yet been translated into English, but excerpts were published in 1935 (Von Lama).

Mechtilde saw angels clearly and in full color. She said that the guardian angels of innocent souls wear white and the guardian angels of children often wear blue. Guardian angels of people who suffer greatly in this incarnation wear crimson clothes and a crown (Connell, 100).

St. Mary Magdalene de Pazzi (1566–1607) had an unusual vision in which she saw not only her own guardian angel but also the guardian angels of the other nuns in her convent. In the vision, she walked into a beautiful garden where the nuns' guardian angels were weaving crowns of flowers. All the crowns were different and featured a variety of different colors that reflected the qualities each soul possessed. Jesus appeared to her and told her that if the souls lacked charity, their guardian angels would not be able to make the crowns of flowers (Minima, 47–48).

I've met many people who are able to see other people's guardian angels, and their descriptions vary considerably. Only a few of them see guardian angels in different colors, and they appear to correspond with the main color that is visible in their charges' auras. It's possible that these people and Mechtilde were seeing the person's aura while looking at the guardian angel. It's also possible (and not that surprising) that the color of the guardian angel's clothes happens to be the same color as the person's aura. In either case, the main color of the aura, known as the ground color, indicates the most important lesson the person has to learn in this lifetime.

Knowing another person's most important lesson helps you enormously when dealing with that person. If you wanted someone to happily take on a challenge involving a great deal of hard work, you'd choose someone who had a guardian angel dressed in green. If you wanted to do something exciting or adventurous, you'd choose someone whose guardian angel wore blue clothes to do it with you. If you needed someone to look after your investments, someone with an angel wearing silver would be a good choice. Obviously, you need to look at other aspects of the person's character as well, but this gives you a good start.

Here are the most important lessons for each color:

Red

Keywords: Independence and attainment

People with guardian angels dressed in red need to learn to stand on their own two feet and achieve independence. They often start out in life by being dependent and are sometimes forced to learn the lesson of independence. Once this lesson has been learned, they can use their leadership skills, creative talents, and potential for accomplishment to achieve anything they desire. This frequently includes financial reward.

Orange

Keywords: Harmony and cooperation

People who have guardian angels dressed in orange are good at harmonizing and working well with others. They are good contributors but don't always receive the recognition or credit they deserve. They are sensitive and easily hurt. Once they learn how to handle this, they receive a great deal of love and friendship in this incarnation.

Yellow

Keywords: Self-expression and sociability

People with guardian angels dressed in yellow need to learn the joy of self-expression. They are usually positive people with good imaginations and creative capabilities. They are talented with words, which makes them good conversationalists. They can also express themselves well as actors, singers, professional speakers, writers, and any other career that utilizes their verbal skills. They sometimes need to learn motivation to make the most of their talents.

Green

Keywords: Practicality and service

People with guardian angels dressed in green need to learn the benefits of system and order in accomplishing their goals. They need to work in harmony with the limitations and restraints that life puts them through. They are honest, sincere, conscientious, hard-working, and patient. They can be rigid and stubborn at times, but only when they feel it is necessary to put their point of view across.

Blue

Keywords: Change and variety

People with guardian angels dressed in blue need to learn how to use their time wisely and constructively. They are active, versatile, restless, and enthusiastic people who see exciting possibilities everywhere. They enjoy change and need constant variety in their lives. Because of this, they find it hard to handle routine tasks and get bored easily.

Indigo

Keywords: Love and responsibility

People whose guardian angels wear indigo-colored clothes need to learn how to handle responsibility. They enjoy nurturing and caring for people who need help and support. Unfortunately, others can sometimes take advantage of this generosity. They are loving, friendly, appreciative, sympathetic, and kind. They are usually the one people come to when they need help and advice.

Violet

Keywords: Wisdom and understanding

People with guardian angels dressed in violet need to develop inwardly and develop their spiritual awareness and intuition. This is a nonmaterialistic path. They need to handle being on their own without feeling lonely and use this time to develop their considerable knowledge and wisdom. These people have a different approach, which can make it hard for other people to understand them.

Silver

Keywords: Materialism and attainment

People with guardian angels dressed in silver need to learn how to work in the material world and appreciate the rewards that come as a result of their hard work and organizational ability. They are confident, ambitious, reliable, practical, and stubborn. Once they've achieved their financial goals, they need to use their wealth and power wisely.

Gold

Keywords: Humanitarianism and universal love

People with guardian angels dressed in gold need to learn how to give of themselves without any thought of personal reward. They need to be selfless and give love, assistance, and understanding to anyone who needs it. Their satisfaction must come from the sheer joy of giving. They are sensitive, compassionate, sympathetic, tolerant, and idealistic. This is a difficult lesson, but the rewards are immeasurable.

Pink

Keywords: Love and peace

People with guardian angels dressed in pink need to learn how to make use of their love, innocence, compassion, and sensitivity in a world that doesn't always appreciate these valuable qualities. They'll be hurt many times, but must learn to get up again and continue shining their purity and compassion on everyone they encounter. It is a difficult road, but a powerful one for people who want to make a difference in the world.

CHAPTER FIVE
PRAYERS AND BLESSINGS

When life becomes difficult, it can be hard for even the most positive of people to realize how blessed they are. Fortunately, you're always surrounded by angels who are willing to help and guide you. You can perform an angel blessing ritual whenever you wish. It can be helpful to do this even in good times, as the ritual will remind you of just how many blessings you have in your life. You can perform a blessing ritual to help anyone who needs it. You can also perform an angel blessing for a group of people. I regularly perform group angel blessings, both in person and online, and have been fortunate enough to perform these for up to a thousand people at a time.

If you're performing an angel blessing ritual for yourself, make a list ahead of time of all the blessings you enjoy in your life. You list might include:

- The gift of life—The fact that you're alive right now is a priceless gift.
- Your physical body and health—Think about the gifts of sight, hearing, taste, smell. Think also about your voice and the ability to communicate. Think about your legs that carry you from place to place. Your arms, hands, and fingers can do many varied tasks, from lifting

to caressing and even healing. Your heart pumps blood throughout your body every moment of your life.

- Your mind—It gives you intelligence, thoughts, and creativity.
- Your soul—It provides you with a direct link to the Divine.
- The special people in your life—You might include parents, siblings, your partner, children, grandchildren, and friends. These people help you every day with their love and acceptance. Your list might also include doctors, nurses, teachers, and people who serve you in stores and other places you visit.
- Your guardian angel—For protecting and guiding you throughout all your incarnations.
- Your ability to communicate with specific angels whenever you need specialized help.
- Your home that provides you with shelter and a place to live.
- Your work that supplies you with an income as well as opportunities to learn, grow, and progress.
- The hobbies and interests that provide you with pleasure and fulfillment.

You might also list tangible items, such as investments, money in the bank, and your car. You could list intangible items, too, such as your faith, intuition, good taste, and luck.

You can move further outside yourself and think about the advantages of living where you live, in addition to the facilities and opportunities that exist in your neighborhood, town, and country.

It can be useful to regularly create a list of all the blessings in your life to help you live with feelings of gratitude and abundance. When I worked as a hypnotherapist, I regularly suggested to clients who came for insomnia to think about the blessings in their lives when they went to bed. This took their minds away from their problems and concerns, and in many cases helped them relax enough to fall asleep.

THE RITUAL

There are four parts to the angel blessing. The first part is creating an invisible circle of protection around yourself. Once that has been done, you perform a clearing on yourself. This is to release any negativity that might be surrounding you and to enhance positivity. The third part is the angel blessing, and the final part is to end the ritual by thanking the four major archangels and releasing the circle.

Preparation

Find a relaxing environment to perform the angel blessing in. The room needs to be pleasantly warm, and your clothes should be loose-fitting and comfortable. You might want to play some gentle New Age music to set the mood.

If you have a pendulum, place it nearby so you can use it in the personal clearing section.

You'll also need about thirty minutes of uninterrupted time to perform the blessing.

How to Create the Circle of Protection

Start the ritual by performing the Angelic Invocation of Protection from chapter 3. You can create a circle around you wherever you happen to be. If you're sitting in an armchair, all you need do is imagine a circle that completely surrounds you and the chair. If you're lying down in bed, imagine a circle that consists of a semi-circle in the air above you, and a semicircle that goes under the bed, and maybe even the floor. The two semicircles are joined to create your magic circle. I prefer to use a chair with a straight back placed in the center of the room I'm working in. I stand while creating the circle and then sit down for the blessing. I stand up again to release the circle at the end of the ritual.

Personal Clearing

The second part of the ritual is to give yourself a personal clearing. I usually do this with a pendulum, but you can make the negative and positive movements with your dominant hand if you don't happen to have one with you.

Swing your pendulum (or move your hand in small circles) in a counterclockwise direction while saying, preferably out loud:

"I ask (God, Divine Spirit, Universal Life Force, or whatever term you choose to use) and the angels to release any negativity that is adversely affecting me in any way. Please release all the negativity in my body, mind, and spirit. Please release any negativity in all the environments I find myself within today. Please also release any negativity that might be trapped inside the bodies, minds, and hearts of all the people I love. Please allow any negativity I encounter today to totally dissolve and lose any power to harm me or anyone else, in any way. Please, (God, Divine Spirit, Universal Life Force, etc.), replace all the negativity with peace, harmony, and divine love."

Think of your intent and watch your pendulum until it stops moving. Once it stops, swing it in a clockwise direction (or move your dominant hand in clockwise circles) and say:

"I ask the angels for peace of mind, happiness, joy, and love in everything I do today. Help me spread joy and happiness everywhere I go, so that everyone I encounter will feel better as a result of my presence. Please help me be courteous, patient, kind, and understanding, even in difficult situations. Please help me make a positive difference for everyone I encounter today.

"Please strengthen my aura so I can deflect any anxiety, stress, fear, and any other form of negativity I might encounter yet remain open to everything positive and good. Please help me see the good in everyone I meet.

"Please bless any food and drink I consume, and allow it to nurture my body, mind, and spirit. Please eliminate any disease from my physical body, so I can enjoy radiant health and vitality. Please help me become the person I want to be. Thank you. Thank you. Thank you."

Again, watch the movements of the pendulum until it stops. When it does, say one final thank-you.

Pendulums are usually used for dowsing, which means they can detect anything hidden, such as oil, water, or precious minerals. However, they can also be used for other purposes, such as answering questions, encouraging spiritual healing, and setting intentions. This personal clearing uses a pendulum to set an intention, and to eliminate negativity and attract positivity.

If you don't have a pendulum, you can use your dominant hand to do these things for you. Move your hand in small counterclockwise circles while saying the first part of the clearing (removing negativity), and in clockwise circles (to enhance positivity) while saying the second half.

You are now fully protected by the four archangels, and have eliminated negativity and attracted positivity into your life. We're finally ready to move on to the angel blessing.

ANGEL BLESSING

The angel blessing is a guided meditation in which you'll connect with angelic energy, especially that of your guardian angel. Make yourself as comfortable as you can, close your eyes, and relax. You can use any method you like to completely relax your body. If I'm short on time, I'll silently count from five down to one and then allow every cell in my body to relax. Most of the time, I use a progressive relaxation that takes about five minutes. You might find it helpful to record the words I use. Alternatively, read them two or three times and then close your eyes and silently go through the process using a mixture of your words and mine until you feel completely relaxed.

"Take a nice deep breath in, and close your eyes as you exhale. Let all your muscles relax. Allow yourself to go deeper and deeper into pleasant relaxation with every breath you take. It's a wonderful feeling to simply let yourself go and drift into a pleasant, peaceful, relaxed state. It's so calm, so quiet, and so, so relaxing.

"And as you're relaxing more and more, become aware of Raphael, Michael, Gabriel, and Uriel, the four great archangels, surrounding you with love and protection. Knowing they're with you helps you drift even deeper into pleasant relaxation. Allow the sound of my voice to mix with each breath you take and relax even more. Enjoy the feeling of total relaxation drifting into every part of your body, from the top of your head to the tips of your toes.

"You can keep on going deeper now. Notice how comfortable and relaxed you feel as you drift even deeper into pleasant relaxation. Notice how relaxed your feet feel, and allow that pleasant relaxation to drift up into your legs, allowing all the muscles in your calves and thighs to let go more and more. Feel the relaxation drifting up into your abdomen and chest, and down each arm into your hands and fingers. Allow all the muscles in your shoulders and neck to relax, and let this wonderful sense of relaxation into your head and face. Feel the fine muscles round your eyes relaxing, too. So pleasant, so peaceful, and so relaxing.

"As you're breathing deeply, and relaxing more and more with every breath, simply enjoy this wonderful feeling of complete and total relaxation spreading into every cell of your body. It's an amazing feeling to be safe, protected, loved, and so, so relaxed.

"In your imagination, visualize a beautiful white light descending and surrounding you with its gentle, restorative, healing energy. Each breath you take fills you with this divine love and energy.

"Now visualize Archangel Raphael standing in front of you as part of your circle of protection. He has a huge smile on his face as he steps forward, gives you a hug, and then places his right hand on top of your head. He asks you to take a deep breath and let go of any negative feelings or emotions you might have as you exhale. Raphael tells you to let go of all negativity. As you do, you can feel a sense of lightness in your entire body as you eliminate all the pains and hurts you've been carrying for so long. You no longer need them, and with Raphael's help, you know you've let them go. You feel totally at peace. Archangel Raphael hugs you again and then steps back to complete the circle of protection. You silently thank him and he smiles again.

"Now you see Archangel Michael step toward you. He also gives you a hug and then places his right hand on your shoulder. You sense his strength and love and instantly know that all your fears, doubts, and worries have disappeared. You also get a strong sense of knowing that he is ready and willing to protect you whenever you ask for it. He hugs you again and then steps back. You silently thank him for looking after you and keeping you safe.

"You realize that Archangel Gabriel, who was behind you, is now standing in front of you. He gives you a hug, too. Instead of standing back again, he continues to hug you, and you feel yourself totally surrounded in his love and care for you. You instinctively realize that whenever you need guidance, Gabriel will be there to help you. Gabriel tightens the hug for a moment and then disappears. You somehow know that he's standing behind you again, completing the circle of protection.

"On your left side, Archangel Uriel stands forward. He also hugs you and then places his right hand on your left shoulder. You immediately feel a sense of peace and tranquility flow through you. You can sense all past pain and trauma dissipating and disappearing with his gentle yet powerful touch. Uriel quietly tells you that he wants you to experience the same divine light that he gives to mystics, explaining that it will help you gain a closer connection with the Divine. He hugs you again and steps back.

"In this quiet and peaceful relaxed state, become aware of all the blessings in your life. Think of them, one by one, and give thanks to God (Divine Spirit, Universal Life Force, etc.) for giving you the gift of life, and for all the other blessings you enjoy. We usually take these blessings for granted, and it feels good to thank the Creator of the Universe for them. Take as long as you wish. While you're doing this, you may sense the presence of angels. It might be a soft movement that you can barely detect. It could be a gentle touch on your arm or cheek. You might sense a beautiful perfume. If you're very fortunate, you might receive a gentle caress from the wings of an angel, most probably your guardian angel.

"Pause now, and send some thoughts to your guardian angel. Thank your guardian angel for being with you, and for surrounding you with love and support from the moment you were born. Ask your guardian angel if they have a message for you. Continue to relax and give your angel time to send you a message. It might appear as a sudden, unexpected thought. It might be a feeling, a sense of knowing what you're supposed to be doing with your life. You might hear your guardian angel quietly talking to you. You might picture your guardian angel in your mind's eye. Angel messages can come in all sorts of different ways. If you receive nothing now, remain confident that you'll receive a message very soon, maybe in your dreams tonight or some other way. Know that beyond a shadow of a doubt, your guardian angel is always with you. Promise your angel that you'll try to be more attentive to what they are trying to say.

"You might want to ask questions about matters in your life. You can ask anything you wish. It's a good way to start a conversation with your angel. Listen attentively to the answers. The replies will probably appear as thoughts in your mind.

"You should certainly ask for help in gaining anything lacking in your life. Ask for health, happiness, love, abundance, and anything else you desire. There are angels who look after different areas of life, and your guardian angel will introduce you to them if necessary.

"Remember also that right now you're surrounded by God's most powerful archangels, and you can speak directly to them. You can communicate with Archangel Raphael for any matters involving spiritual, emotional, mental, and physical healing. Talk with Archangel Michael if you need courage, strength, or protection. Call on Michael if you're tempted to be anything less than honest. Talk with Archangel Gabriel if you have doubts, fears, and worries. Gabriel will also provide guidance, purification, and forgiveness. A conversation with Archangel Uriel will provide you with a whole new perspective on life. He'll help you find inner peace and tranquility, clarity and insight, and will also help you develop your psychic and intuitive skills. In addition to all that, Archangel Uriel wants you to prosper and lead a successful, fulfilled life.

"Once you've spoken to the angels you need at this time, ask for an angelic blessing. Visualize the four archangels providing a circle of protection around you, and sense your guardian angel inside that circle, surrounding you with pure, unconditional love. In your imagination, look up and see that you're totally surrounded by angels everywhere you look. The sky is full of myriads of angels, and they're all smiling at you. They're telling you that they love you unconditionally and that they're always there for you. They want to help you make the most of this incarnation. Right now, they want to send you extra blessings and reassure you that you can always call on them for help and guidance. As you're surrounded with all this divine love, sense the area around your heart open up to receive this wonderful blessing from the angelic realms. Allow this amazing energy to flow into every cell of your body, revitalizing, restoring, and blessing it fully.

"You realize that with the help of your angels, you can achieve anything. You feel a new sense of power, and maybe for the first time, you become aware of your unlimited potential. You deserve happiness, love, fulfillment, and abundance. Ask the angels to help you claim what you so rightfully deserve. Spend a few moments enjoying the blessing, the unconditional love of all the angels, and the recognition of you as a vital, important part of the entire universe. You feel truly blessed.

"And now, thank the angels for everything they have done, are doing, and will do for you. Tell them what they mean to you and how much you appreciate their work on your behalf. The choirs of angels gradually fade from sight, and now you're surrounded by the four archangels. Express your gratitude to them for everything they do for you, and thank them for protecting you during this angel blessing. Thank Archangel Uriel, followed by Gabriel, Michael, and Raphael. As they fade from view, you sense your guardian angel standing in front of you. Thank them, and then silently count from one to five. Open your eyes. The blessing is over."

DAILY BLESSINGS

With your guardian angel's help, you can improve many people's lives by silently blessing them everywhere you go. As well as helping others, you'll improve the quality of your own life every time you give a blessing. When you think negatively, you unconsciously send out negative messages to others. It's impossible to send out good, positive blessings when you're full of negative thoughts such as anger, bitterness, or resentment. Consequently, sending out positive blessings to others keeps you in a positive state of mind. It's a good example of reaping what you sow.

All you need do is to ask your guardian angel to help you send out blessings to others. When you wake up in the morning, tell your guardian angel that you intend to bless at least one thousand people today. Ask if your angel is willing to help you. Once you have your angel's approval, think of the many blessings you have in your life as you prepare for the day ahead.

Start by silently sending a blessing to the first person you encounter. Visualize your guardian angel standing beside you. With their encouragement, silently say something simple, such as, "I bless you." You might prefer to prefer to say something along the lines of: "I surround you with love and happiness. I wish you all the best that life has to offer." You'll probably never know the effect your blessing has on this person, but you'll feel a boost in your own positivity and happiness.

If you travel to work on a bus or train, ask your guardian angel to help you send a blessing to everyone traveling on it. You can send a blessing to the occupants of the car in front of you when you're driving. Make sure to send blessings to everyone at places where you shop or visit regularly. Bless all your colleagues at work, even the ones who constantly annoy you. In fact, those people should receive a personal blessing rather than a group one.

When you pass a hospital, send a blessing to everyone who works there as well as all the patients. You can bless all the teachers and students when you pass a school. You can bless people at the clubs and organizations you belong to. You can bless the occupants of a plane you see high above you. You can bless people who appear on your television screen or whose voices you hear on the radio.

Every now and again during the day, let your guardian angel know how you're getting on and approximately how many people you've blessed. There's no limit to the number of people you can bless. You might bless everyone attending a football game or a rock concert. You can send blessings to people in faraway countries, especially those who are suffering. There are no limitations to whom you can bless or how far away they happen to be.

This exercise will help you in many ways. It will increase your own positivity and the connection you have with your guardian angel. And because we become what we think about, it will increase the quality of every aspect of your life.

There is no limit to what you can bless. You can bless animals, food, drink, the world, and even yourself. Whenever you feel upset, stressed, or unhappy for any reason, ask your guardian angel to help you give yourself a blessing, too.

PRAYER OF THE HEART WITH YOUR GUARDIAN ANGEL

It takes time and practice to gain expertise at contemplative prayer. However, it's worth persevering, as it has many rewards. The main benefit is that you'll spend time in the presence of the Divine, accompanied by your guardian angel. You'll nurture your soul and feel an increased sense of well-being and happiness. You'll get a powerful glimpse of the perfection and mystery of the universe. As a byproduct, your health will benefit, as your stress levels and blood pressure will decrease.

Set aside at least forty minutes where you won't be disturbed.

1. Start by performing the Angelic Invocation of Protection in chapter 3.

2. Sit down comfortably, close your eyes, and take three slow, deep breaths. Visualize your guardian angel standing beside you, and "see" you both smiling at each other.

3. Relax your body, starting by focusing on your left foot and toes. Allow the muscles in your left foot to relax completely and then allow the pleasant relaxation to drift over your ankles and into your calf muscles. When they've relaxed, allow the relaxation to drift over your knee and into your thighs. Repeat this with your right toes, foot, and leg.

4. Once both legs are relaxed, allow the relaxation to drift into your abdomen and chest, followed by your shoul-

ders, arms, hands, and fingers. Allow the relaxation to spread through your neck, and move up into your face before relaxing the rest of your head.

5. Mentally scan your entire body to make sure that you are completely relaxed. Relax any areas that are still tense, and feel a gentle touch from your guardian angel which tells you that you're completely relaxed and able to continue.

6. Think of the most beautiful, peaceful place you've ever seen, and visualize you and your guardian angel inside the scene. Take three slow, deep breaths, visualizing this scene with each breath.

7. Forget about your breathing, but continue visualizing you and your guardian angel in the beautiful setting. Wait silently and expectantly. Every time a random thought comes into your mind, dismiss it gently. You might like to imagine yourself placing the thought onto a fluffy cloud and watching it drift away. It's natural for stray thoughts to drift into your mind while praying contemplatively.

8. Each time you dismiss an unwanted thought, direct your mind back to peace and quiet. You might return to the beautiful scene with your guardian angel. You might prefer to simply be, and sit quietly, waiting to hear from the Divine.

9. Stay for as long as you can in this quiet, meditative, contemplative state. You may find a few minutes are all you can manage when you first try this.

10. When you feel ready, smile at your guardian angel. Take three slow, deep breaths, become familiar with

your surroundings, and thank and dismiss the four great archangels. Count from one to five, open your eyes, and spend a few minutes thinking about your contemplative prayer before getting up. Make sure to write down any insights or thoughts that came to you during or after your prayer.

11. Repeat this prayer as often as you can. The more you practice, the better you'll become, and the easier it will be to perform.

CONCLUSION

I hope you've performed some of the rituals and visualizations in this book and strengthened your connection with both your guardian angel and the Divine. Your angel will greatly appreciate all of the rituals and visualizations you perform, as you are your guardian angel's sole purpose.

In the hustle and bustle of everyday life, it can be easy to forget that there's more to life than the material world we live in. Sadly, many people lead their entire lives in the material world and pay no attention to the spiritual side of their being. One of my favorite quotes is: "We are not human beings having a spiritual experience; we are spiritual beings having a human experience." These words, attributed to two of my heroes—Pierre Teilhard de Chardin and G. I. Gurdjieff—show the importance of the spiritual side of life. Most people know, possibly on an unconscious level, that we're not simply the sum total of our thoughts and feelings. We're aware that we're part of something larger than ourselves and that, in some way, we're all connected to the Godhead, or divine essence, however or whatever we perceive that to be.

Many people discover their divine connection when experiencing something they can't explain. When they tell others about it, they usually start with: "Something told me not to…" or "I just had a feeling…." By following the voice's instructions, these people might have avoided a traffic accident or some other potentially dangerous situation. They may have overcome a temptation to do something wrong. They might have suddenly thought of a dear friend and, after calling them, discovered they needed help. Now that you've read this book, do you think it's possible that this quiet voice may have been their guardian angel looking after them?

My life changed enormously after my guardian angel spoke to me for the first time when I was going through a difficult time in early adulthood. Over the years, I've met many people who were contacted by their guardian angels for the first time when they were overwhelmed with problems and worries.

Recently, a lady told me that her first contact with her guardian angel occurred when she was extremely happy. She had been married for two years and was expecting her first baby. "Life was so good," she told me, "that I started doing the blessing you told me about. It made me feel even happier, and then my guardian angel appeared, first in a dream, and then every time I did a blessing. I talk with her several times every day." The blessing she's referring to is in chapter 5.

Your guardian angel is ready to communicate with you at any time. It doesn't matter if you're happy or sad, rich or poor, in a relationship or on your own, or anything else.

Fortunately, your guardian angel wants to have a closer connection with you, which means you can start communicating with your angel whenever you wish. Communication often happens when people are ready to explore the spiritual aspects of their life.

In the overall scheme of things, it doesn't matter how or when you meet your guardian angel. What is important is that you make that connection with your closest friend. I hope this book helps you to develop a close bond and a deep friendship with your guardian angel.

Bibliography

The Apocrypha. Revised version. Cambridge, UK: Cambridge University Press, 1983. First published 1895 by Oxford University Press (Oxford, UK).

Ali, Abdullah Yusuf, trans. *The Qur'an*. Elmhurst, NY: Tahrike Tarile Qur'an, Inc., 2001.

Adam, James. *The Vitality of Platonism*. Cambridge, UK: Cambridge University Press, 1911.

Bede, The Venerable. *A History of the English Church and People*. Translated by Leo Sherley-Price and R. E. Latham. Harmondsworth, UK: Penguin Books, 1996.

Black, Jonathan. *The Sacred History: How Angels, Mystics and Higher Intelligence Made Our World*. London: Quercus Editions Limited, 2013.

Bonaventure. *The Works of Bonaventure: Cardinal, Seraphic Doctor and Saint*. Volumes 1–5. Translated by José de Vinck. Paterson, NJ: St. Anthony Guild Press, 1960–69.

Brewer, E. Cobham. *A Dictionary of Miracles: Imitative, Realistic, and Dogmatic*. London: Chatto and Windus, 1884.

Bruno, Anthony Vincent. *The Wisdom of the Saints*. Accessed 2019 online. https://books.google.co.nz/books?id

=Hp-qDwAAQBAJ&printsec=frontcover&source=gbs
_atb&redir_esc=y#v=onepage&q&f=false.

Byrne, Lorna. *Angels at My Fingertips*. London: Coronet, 2017.

———. *Angels in My Hair*. London: Century, 2008.

———. *Love from Heaven*. London: Coronet, 2014.

———. *A Message of Hope from the Angels*. London: Coronet, 2012.

———. *My Guardian Angel, My Best Friend: Seven Stories for Children*. London: Coronet, 2020.

———. *Prayers from the Heart*. London: Coronet, 2020.

———. *Stairways to Heaven*. London: Coronet, 2012.

———. *The Year with Angels*. London: Coronet, 2016.

Caesarius of Heisterbach. *The Dialogue on Miracles*. Volumes 1 and 2. Translated by H. von Scott and C. C. Swinton Bland. London: G. Routledge and Sons, 1929.

Carpenter, Humphrey. *The Letters of J. R. R. Tolkien*. Boston: Houghton Mifflin-Harcourt, 2014.

Charles, R. H. *The Apocrypha and Pseudepigrapha of the Old Testament*. Oxford, UK: Clarendon Press, 1913.

Chase, Steven. *Angelic Spirituality: Medieval Perspectives on the Ways of Angels*. Mahwah, NJ: Paulist Press, 2002.

Connell, Janice T. *Angel Power*. New York: Ballantine Books, 1995.

Copen, Bruce. *The Practical Pendulum*. Sussex, UK: Academic Publications, 1974.

Crowley, Aleister. *The Book of the Law*. New York, NY: Samuel Weiser, 1976. Originally published privately in 1909.

————. *The Equinox of the Gods*. New York: Gordon Press, 1974. Originally published 1919 as *The Equinox*, volume III, number 3 (London: Ordo Templi Orientis).

————. *Portable Darkness: An Aleister Crowley Reader*. New York: Harmony Books, 1989.

————. *Magick Without Tears*. St. Paul, MN: Llewellyn Publications, 1974. Originally published 1954 by The Thelema Publishing Company (Hampton, NJ).

Daniel, Alma, Timothy Wyllie, and Andrew Ramer. *Ask Your Angels*. New York: Random House, 1992.

Davidson, Gustav. *A Dictionary of Angels: Including the Fallen Angels*. New York: The Free Press, 1967.

De Mello, Anthony. *Taking Flight: A Book of Story Meditations*. New York: Doubleday and Co., 1990.

Dhalla, Maneckji. *History of Zoroastrianism*. Oxford, UK: Oxford University Press, 1938.

Eason, Cassandra. *Encyclopedia of Magic and Ancient Wisdom*. London: Judy Piatkus, 2000.

Fernandez-Carvajal, Francis. *In Conversation with God: Meditation for Each Day of the Year*. Volume 7. Strongsville, OH: Scepter Publishers, 2005.

Fodor, Nandor. *Encyclopaedia of Psychic Science*. London: Arthurs Press, 1933. Reprinted 1966 by University Books (New Hyde Park, NY).

Ginzberg, Louis. *Legends of the Jews*. Translated by Henrietta Szold. Philadelphia: The Jewish Publication Society, 2003. Originally published in seven volumes in 1909, 1910, 1911, 1913, 1925, 1928, and 1938.

Harpur, Patrick. *A Complete Guide to the Soul*. London: Rider, an imprint of Ebury Publishing, 2010.

Hillman, James. *The Soul's Code: In Search of Character and Calling*. New York: Ballantine Books, 1996.

Huber, Georges. *My Angel Will Go Before You*. Translated by Michael Adams. Dublin, IE: Four Courts Press, 1983.

Jeffrey, Francis. *John Lilly, So Far*. Los Angeles: Jeremy P. Tarcher, 1990.

Jovanovik, Pierre. *An Inquiry into the Existence of Guardian Angels*. Translated by Stephen Becker. New York: M. Evans and Company, 1995. Originally published 1993 by Editions Filipacchi (Levallois-Perret, France).

Keck, David. *Angels and Angelology in the Middle Ages*. New York: Oxford University Press, 1998.

Laurence, Richard, translator. *The Book of Enoch the Prophet*. San Diego: Wizard's Bookshelf, 1976. Originally published 1821 by Kegan Paul, Trench & Co. (London).

Lilly, John C. *The Scientist: A Metaphysical Autobiography*. Berkeley, CA: Ronin Publishing, 1988.

Lombard, Peter. *The Sentences, Book 2: On Creation*. Toronto: Pontifical Institute of Mediaeval Studies, 2008.

Mathers, S. L. MacGregor, trans. *The Book of the Sacred Magic of Abramelin the Mage*. Mineola, NY: Dover Publications, 2012. First published 1900 by John M. Watkins (London).

Minima, Sr. Mary. *Seraph Among Angels: The Life of St. Mary Magdalene de' Pazzi*. Chicago, IL: The Carmelite Press, 1958.

Moore, Tom T. *The Gentle Way III: Master Your Life*. Flagstaff, AZ: 3 Light Technology Publishing, 2013.

Thomas Nelson Bibles. *The Holy Bible in the King James Version*. Nashville: Thomas Nelson Publishers, 1984.

Origen. Edited by Alexander Roberts, James Donaldson, and Cleveland A. Coxe. *The Anti-Nicene Fathers*. Volume 4. Peabody, MA: Hendrickson Publishers, 1994.

Parente, Alessio. *Send Me Your Guardian Angel*. Amsterdam, NY: The Noteworthy Company, 1984.

Parisen, Maria. *Angels & Mortals: Their Co-Creative Power*. Wheaton, IL: The Theosophical Publishing House, 1990.

Plato. *Symposium*. Many editions available.

Potter, Richard, and Jan Potter. *Spiritual Development for Beginners*. Woodbury, MN: Llewellyn Publications, 2006.

Pseudo-Dionysius. *Pseudo-Dionysius: The Complete Works*. Translated by Colm Luibheid. Mahwah, NJ: Paulist Press, 1987.

Rees, Valery. *From Gabriel to Lucifer: A Cultural History of Angels*. London: I. B. Taurus & Co., 2013.

Roberts, Ursula. *The Mystery of the Human Aura*. York Beach, ME: Samuel Weiser, 1984. Originally published 1950 by The Spiritualist Association of Great Britain (London).

Ronner, John. *Know Your Angels: The Angel Almanac with Biographies of More than 100 Angels in Legend and Folklore*. Murfreesboro, TN: Mamre Press, 1993.

Sitchin, Zecharia. *Divine Encounters: A Guide to Visions, Angels, and Other Emissaries*. New York: Avon Books, 1995.

Skilling, Johanna. "J. R. R. Tolkien: Love Individualized." In *The Big Book of Angels*. Emmaus, PA: Rodale, 2002.

Smythe, F. S. *Camp Six*. London: Hodder & Stoughton Ltd., 1937.

Stanford, Peter. *Angels: A Visible and Invisible History*. London: Hodder & Stoughton Ltd., 2019.

Von Hochheim, Eckhart. "Sermon Nine." In *The Reading and Preaching of the Scriptures in the Worship of the Christian Church* by Hughes Oliphant Old. Vol. 3, *The Medieval Church*. Grand Rapids, MI: Wm. B. Eerdmans Publishing Company, 1998.

Von Lama, Freidrich, ed. *The Angels, Our God Given Companions and Servants*. Collegeville, MN: Rev. Celestine Kapsner. O.S.B., St. John's Abbey, 1935.

Webster, Richard. *Angels for Beginners*. Woodbury, MN: Llewellyn Publications, 2017.

———. *How to Use a Pendulum: 50 Practical Rituals and Spiritual Rituals for Clarity and Guidance*. Woodbury, MN: Llewellyn Publications, 2020.

———. *Prayer for Beginners*. Woodbury, MN: Llewellyn Publications, 2009.

———. *Spirit Guides & Angel Guardians: Contact Your Invisible Helpers*. St. Paul, MN: Llewellyn Publications, 1988.

Wilson, Colin. *Aleister Crowley: The Nature of the Beast*. Wellingborough, UK: The Aquarian Press, 1987.

Zaleski, Philip, and Carol Zaleski. *The Fellowship: The Literary Lives of the Inklings*. New York: Farrar, Straus & Giroux, 2015.

Index

To Write to the Author

If you wish to contact the author or would like more information about this book, please write to the author in care of Llewellyn Worldwide Ltd. and we will forward your request. Both the author and publisher appreciate hearing from you and learning of your enjoyment of this book and how it has helped you. Llewellyn Worldwide Ltd. cannot guarantee that every letter written to the author can be answered, but all will be forwarded. Please write to:

Richard Webster
℅ Llewellyn Worldwide
2143 Wooddale Drive
Woodbury, MN 55125-2989

Please enclose a self-addressed stamped envelope for reply, or $1.00 to cover costs. If outside the U.S.A., enclose an international postal reply coupon.

Many of Llewellyn's authors have websites with additional information and resources. For more information, please visit our website at http://www.llewellyn.com.